# For Ourselves and Our Posterity

Critical Historical Encounters

*Series Editors*
James Kirby Martin
David M. Oshinsky
Randy W. Roberts

# For Ourselves and Our Posterity

The Preamble to the Federal Constitution
in American History

PETER CHARLES HOFFER
*The University of Georgia*

New York        Oxford
OXFORD UNIVERSITY PRESS

Oxford University Press is a department of the University of Oxford. It furthers the University's objective of excellence in research, scholarship, and education by publishing worldwide.

Oxford   New York
Auckland   Cape Town   Dar es Salaam   Hong Kong   Karachi
Kuala Lumpur   Madrid   Melbourne   Mexico City   Nairobi
New Delhi   Shanghai   Taipei   Toronto

With offices in
Argentina   Austria   Brazil   Chile   Czech Republic   France   Greece
Guatemala   Hungary   Italy   Japan   Poland   Portugal   Singapore
South Korea   Switzerland   Thailand   Turkey   Ukraine   Vietnam

For titles covered by Section 112 of the US Higher Education Opportunity Act, please visit www.oup.com/us/he for the latest information about pricing and alternate formats.

Published by Oxford University Press.
198 Madison Avenue, New York, New York 10016
http://www.oup.com

**Library of Congress Cataloging-in-Publication Data**

Hoffer, Peter Charles, 1944-
For ourselves and our posterity: the preamble to the Federal Constitution in American history/ Peter Charles Hoffer.
   p. cm.
   Includes bibliographical references and index.
   ISBN 978-0-19-989953-1
   1. United States. Constitution.   2. Constitutional law—United States   3. Constitutional history—United States.   I. Title.
   KF4541.H575 2012
   342.7302'9—dc23                                                          2011053155

Printing number: 9  8  7  6  5  4  3  2  1
Printed in the United States of America
on acid-free paper

# CONTENTS

# EDITORS' FOREWORD

.......................

T he volumes in this Oxford University Press book series focus
on major critical encounters in the American experience. The
word "critical" refers to formative, vital, transforming events
and actions that have had a major impact in shaping the ever-changing
contours of life in the United States. "Encounter" indicates a confrontation or clash, oftentimes but not always contentious in character, but
always full of profound historical meaning and consequence.

In this framework the United States, it can be said, has evolved on
contested ground. Conflict and debate, the clash of peoples and ideas,
have marked and shaped American history. The first Europeans trans-
ported with them cultural assumptions that collided with Native American values and ideas. Africans forced into bondage and carried to America
added another set of cultural beliefs that often were at odds with those of
Native Americans and Europeans. Over the centuries America's diverse
peoples differed on many issues, often resulting in formative conflict that
in turn gave form and meaning to the American experience.

The Critical Historical Encounters series emphasizes formative
episodes in America's contested history. Each volume contains two
fundamental ingredients: a carefully written narrative of the encounter and the consequences, both immediate and long-term, of that
moment of conflict in America's contested history.

As Peter Charles Hoffer masterfully demonstrates in this volume,
one of the most lasting of those moments came over the course of
five days in September 1787. Then, five men serving on an ad hoc

"Committee of Style and Arrangement" to edit the draft of the federal constitution at the Constitutional Convention profoundly recast the wording of the Preamble. In so doing, the committee changed a loose federation of sovereign states into a union and laid out an ambitious program for national governance many years ahead of its time. None of this was predetermined by preceding events. The Preamble and all it came to represent was the unique achievement of a remarkable group of men at a momentous turning point in American history.

We should not be surprised that the Committee of Style had so boldly recast the language of the draft of the Constitution the convention left in their charge. The members of the Committee of Style were as able a collection of American legal and political talent as any in our history. They agreed about the need for a strong central government that served the needs of the entire nation. Having been assigned the task of revising the Constitutional Convention's work, they set about their task with energy and conviction. Gouverneur Morris of New York agreed to act as primary draftsman of the new version. James Madison, Alexander Hamilton, and Rufus King helped. William Samuel Johnson, the chair of the committee, facilitated passage of the revisions on the convention floor.

The story of the Preamble began before the Philadelphia Convention and continues to our own day. Though not questioned at the convention, the Preamble began to draw fire when the document arrived at the state ratification conventions. From the ratification conventions, through the debates on states' rights and slavery in the antebellum years, through a civil war and the Reconstruction of the nation, to the creation of new Progressive and New Deal federal agencies, and finally to the concept of a second constitution empowering rather than limiting government and guaranteeing equality, the Preamble became the centerpiece of a constitution for all the people.

The most remarkable feature of the Preamble was its capacity for growth over time. Over and over again its language proved responsive to new perceptions of liberty and justice. The whole of the Preamble would afford grounds to criticize invidious and exclusive distinctions in the law. Its open-ended clauses made it capable of such expansive readings as the American experience continued to unfold over the generations.

James Kirby Martin
David M. Oshinsky
Randy W. Roberts

# PREFACE

·······················

On a chilly November evening in Philadelphia, the Historical Society of Pennsylvania hosted a reception for the American Society for Legal History. Laid out on tables in the reading room were some of the legal treasures of the Society. One of especial interest to me was Edmund Randolph's personal copy of the printed first draft of the proposed federal Constitution. The "Committee of Detail" distributed it to the delegates to the Constitutional Convention on August 6, 1787. The HSP's copy had Randolph's minor handwritten editorial insertions, an "of" here and there. Presumably he had no need for further editing, as he was one of the document's authors.

Randolph was a Virginia lawyer from a leading family whose inner circle connections and courteous manner had already gained him the attorney general's office and then the governorship of his state, an impressive career path for a man about to celebrate his thirty-fourth birthday. Not the most brilliant of the delegates, he deferred to others when it came to weighing the merits and demerits of any idea. But he was liked by both those who favored a new national government and those who feared it. He himself had mixed feelings about the relative strengths and weaknesses of any national government that the convention might frame. In part to resolve his own doubts, in part to explain to his Virginia constituents what the delegates were doing, in June he had urged the convention that the new frame of government "ought to have a preamble." On July 26, he amplified his original proposal: "The object of our preamble ought to be briefly to declare

viii

that the present federal government is insufficient to the general happiness; that the conviction of this fact gave birth to this Convention; and that the only effectual mode which they can devise for curing this insufficiency is the establishment of a supreme legislative, executive, and judiciary. Let it be next declared that the following are the Constitution and fundamentals of government for the United States." He would have more to say in the coming days, but he was the first to ask for a Preamble.

A lightly altered text of the preamble he proposed was incorporated in the Committee of Detail's revised draft of August 20. It read: "We, the people of the states of New Hampshire, Massachusetts, Rhode Island and Providence Plantations, Connecticut, New York, New Jersey, Pennsylvania, Delaware, Maryland, Virginia, North Carolina, South Carolina, and Georgia, do ordain, declare, and establish, the following Constitution for the government of ourselves and our posterity." Although in Randolph's mind the people were the ultimate source of sovereignty—the essence of all republican government—their agency in political terms was channeled through the states they created during the Revolution. He assumed that the delegates wanted a federation of sovereign republican states, each ceding to a federal government a circumscribed portion of their powers.

But that is not how the Constitution of the United States begins. Instead it reads, "We the People of the United States, in order to form a more perfect Union, establish Justice, insure domestic tranquility, provide for the common defence, promote the general welfare, and secure the blessings of liberty to ourselves and our posterity, do ordain and establish this Constitution for the United States of America." In five days, from September 8th to September 12th, a new five-member "Committee of Style and Arrangement" created a formula for American constitutionalism quite different from Randolph's, a formula that has weathered over two hundred years of partisan contest, economic and geographical expansion, the rise of democracy, and even a civil war. In *For Ourselves and Our Posterity*, I offer an account of how the Preamble came to read as it does, and how its language affected constitutional history in the years that followed its adoption.

................

Many years ago a famous English historian told his students, "never apologize, never explain." Their work should do the talking for them.

This good admonition notwithstanding, a few notes to the reader about the following pages are in order.

First, although I am writing for general readers and students, my subject requires the use of some technical legal language. I have tried to explain these "terms of art" whenever they appear.

As has been my practice in previous works, I try to let my subjects speak for themselves as much as possible. It would be a rare historian indeed who could write with more fire than Alexander Hamilton, greater depth of understanding than James Madison, more self-confidence than Gouverneur Morris, and greater learning than Joseph Story, to name a few of the luminaries who grace the pages that follow. Their words—not mine—infuse the story of the Preamble with its drama, and their power of intellect and political understanding elevate it to its place in American constitutional thinking.

There is a gap in the flow of those primary source works around which I had to navigate. Historians have voluminous evidence of the framers' thinking before and after the Committee of Style and Arrangement crafted the Preamble and reassembled the articles of the Constitution, but I have not found primary source evidence of what the committee members were thinking or saying to one another during those five days. I have tried to fill that gap with the words that the committee members spoke and wrote after they presented the finished product to the convention, but sometimes I found myself relying on surmise and assumption. When I found myself in that situation, I phrased my reading of the evidence with the appropriate tentativeness.

Every historian faces the question whether to present the material in narrative or topical format. This was a problem for me here. Although the general organization of the book is chronological, parts of each chapter emphasize one or more of the clauses of the Preamble. Thus within each chapter there are some topical passages that look backward or forward beyond the immediate chronological narrative.

A word or two about the endnotes: as this is not a monograph, I have tried to keep the number and length of the references to a minimum. Some primary sources, for example passages quoted from the state constitutions, are available at the stroke of a few keys on the internet and need not be cited in the endnotes. Secondary source references for quotations or arguments that are not my own do appear there, supplemented by citations in the further reading section at the end of the book.

Finally, because readers will quickly see that I believe the Preamble's purposes worthy of fulfillment, they may incorrectly regard the following pages as "Whig" legal history. In Whig history, not only does everything improve, it must improve. Progress is an invariant historical rule. The history of the Preamble to the Constitution exhibits no such steady progress of ideals. Not everyone who cited the Preamble took it seriously. Sometimes a reference was mere window dressing or rhetorical bluster. Thus I follow the convoluted path of the ideals embedded in the Preamble from their Revolutionary origins to the uses of the Preamble in our own time.

## Acknowledgments

My journey through these historical materials is now almost a half-century long. I studied the connection between the Revolution and the Constitution as a graduate student at Harvard in the latter part of the 1960s, and returned to these issues when I spent the academic year 1986–1987 at Harvard Law School. Many sessions of the New York University Law School seminar in legal history that Bill Nelson and John Reid led offered invaluable lessons on how legal thinkers address these questions. The addition of Dan Hulsebosch to the crew made a very good thing even better. Working on a book about impeachment with Natalie Hull in the 1970s and 1980s, and on a history of the Supreme Court with Professor Hull and Williamjames Hoffer at the start of the twenty-first century, I was able to revisit the storied battlefields of constitutional thinking. Along the way I encumbered debts (in more or less chronological order) to Bernard Bailyn, Les Benedict, Mike Belknap, Stan Katz, Harold Hyman, Kermit Hall, Cass Sunstein, Terry Fisher, Mort Horwitz, R. B. Bernstein, Paul Finkelman, Wythe Holt, Al Brophy, Mel Urofsky, Bill Wiecek, Laura Kalman, Earl Maltz, Sally Gordon, Maeva Marcus, and the many authors in the University Press of Kansas Landmark Law Cases and American Society series I co-edit with Professor Hull. James Kirby Martin encouraged me to work on this project. Brian Wheel and Sarah Ellerton offered invaluable support. R. B. Bernstein, Rick Beeman, Ed Purcell, and Jack Rakove agreed to read the manuscript at an early stage, as did Natalie Hull and Williamjames Hoffer. A conversation with my colleague Michael Winship when the manuscript was nearly done refocused my own conception of my argument. Readers for Oxford University

Press, including Robert J. Allison, David Brown, R. Blake Dunnavent, Mark F. Fernandez, George W. Geib, Woody Holton, Gabriel Loiacono, James McWilliams, James B. M. Schick, and Karim Tiro, were both kind and instructive in their comments. To all of these fine people, for all they have done, I here express my deepest gratitude.

# INTRODUCTION

························

Over the course of five days in September 1787, five men serving on an ad hoc "Committee of Style and Arrangement" to edit the draft of the federal constitution at the Constitutional Convention profoundly recast the wording of the Preamble. In so doing, the committee changed a federation into a union and laid out an ambitious program for national governance many years ahead of its time. None of this was predetermined by preceding events. The Preamble and all it came to represent was the unique achievement of a remarkable group of men at a momentous turning point in American history.

The authors of the new Preamble did not have to defend it at the Convention. No one objected to its high-minded phraseology, perhaps because no one except the five members of the committee seemed to realize what the Preamble foretold, perhaps because the words themselves seemed familiar. In the states' debates over ratification of the Constitution bits and pieces of the Preamble drew the ire of the anti-federalists, the loose coalition that opposed the Constitution. Still, none of the critics fully comprehended what the Committee of Style had accomplished. In the first years of the new nation, however, officials of the new federal government began to debate the implications of the Preamble. In the formative years of the new nation and into its great testing time—the Civil War and Reconstruction Era—the nation's leaders read the Preamble's promise to "We the People" in contending ways. Those contentions continued into the twentieth century. This is the story of that Preamble.

1

In hindsight one should not be surprised that the Committee of Style had so boldly recast the language of the preamble given them by the Committee of Detail. The Committee of Style boasted a stellar array of talent, boldness, and revolutionary vision. All but one of its members agreed upon the need for a strong national government, and having been assigned the task of revising the Constitutional Convention's work, they set about their task with conviction and éclat. Gouverneur Morris of New York undertook the task of drafting the new version. James Madison, Alexander Hamilton, and Rufus King served as sounding boards. William Samuel Johnson, the chair of the committee, smoothed their path when the finished work was presented to the convention.

Four of the committee members had extensive legal practices. The fifth member, James Madison, had studied law extensively but did not pursue it as a career. All had immense respect for the law and saw the world in terms of law. More and better law was their solution to disorder, uncertainty, and conflict—which made their conduct highly questionable from the moment the convention was called to order, for they had intentionally challenged the letter of the instructions calling them together.

In February 1787, the Congress of the confederation called The United States of America asked the states to send delegates to a Philadelphia conference to recommend amendments to the Articles of Confederation. The Articles created the Congress but gave it no real judicial or fiscal power (though the Congress could mediate legal disputes between states and requisition funds from them), nor any power over individuals within the states. Some of the states had already begun the selection process. Whether the state legislatures charged their delegates with the Congress's instructions or opted for a more thorough program of reform, no government body asked the delegates to throw out the Articles of Confederation and start writing a new constitution. The members of the convention disregarded those instructions the moment they arrived in Philadelphia. The Constitution they crafted was a new document creating a sovereign federal government over the entire nation. The Preamble signaled that departure: "We the people of the United States," not the states or the people of the individual states, ordained and established the new federal Union.

The Committee of Style's bold assertion of "We the People" as the government's final source of authority is today synonymous with the American nation, but before the Constitution was adopted Americans were not unified in their thinking about national government. While most shared a pride in their independence and looked forward to a prosperous future, politically they were citizens of states allied in a confederation. The states in that confederation did not always trust one another. New York and Pennsylvania imposed economic debilities on New Jersey. Rhode Island's deflated paper currency undermined Massachusetts' merchants' commercial dealings. Virginia and North Carolina land speculators wrangled about their respective claims to western land, as did Connecticut and Pennsylvania land development companies. Nor did the people of the states regard one another in neighborly fashion. Connecticut's Noah Webster smirked at the "microscopic minds" of ordinary southerners. Years later, actress Fanny Kemble came away from a visit to Charleston, South Carolina, complaining that the great planters there were "idle, arrogant, ignorant, and dissolute." In their turn, southerners were suspicious of New England religious bigotry and infuriated by the smug moralism of the New Englanders.[1]

Nor were the drafters of the Preamble typical of "We the People." Instead, they were a select number of well educated, well to do, well respected men chosen for their task by state legislators themselves high in social and economic status. The state ratification conventions' 1,648 delegates shared the social, economic, religious and demographic bias of the fifty-five members of the Philadelphia convention. Some were more democratic in their outlook than others, and some were more conservative, but these ideological distinctions (revealed in their sometimes raucous debates over the Constitution) do not obscure the fact that they were overwhelmingly white, Protestant, property-owning, English-speaking men.

All of these men believed that republican government was founded upon consent of the governed. The revolutionary states' constitutions professed adherence to this principle. But in fact many Americans did not take any part in the process by which state constitutions were framed and legislatures were chosen. Women (except for a brief period in New Jersey), servants, slaves, Indians, newcomers, and in many states Catholics and Jews were not permitted to vote. As Susan B. Anthony fumed to a convention of supporters of female suffrage, nearly a century after the ratification of the Constitution, "The preamble of the Federal Constitution says: 'We, *the people* of the United States, in order to form a more perfect union, establish justice, insure domestic tranquillity, provide for the common defence, promote the general welfare, and *secure* the blessings of liberty to ourselves and our posterity, do ordain and establish this Constitution for the United States of America." It was *we the people*—not we *white male citizens*—nor yet we *male citizens*—but we the *whole people*, who formed this Union; and we formed it, not to *give* the blessings of liberty, but to *secure* them—not to the *half* of ourselves and the half of our posterity, but to the whole people, *women* as well as men." Even among white men who could vote, there were rumbles of "disappointment" with the state constitutional convention delegations.[2]

What gave the framers of the Preamble the authority to write "We the People" if they were not typical of the people, representative of the people, or even chosen by the people? The historical answer is that "We the People" and the following clauses of the Preamble were rooted in the common experience of a polity. History, not democracy, elevated a ruling elite to their law-giving role. In an "expanding, aggressive, and calculating society" upwardly mobile men like Rufus King of Massachusetts and Alexander Hamilton of New York had found that chance, ability, ambition, and picking the right side at the right time could elevate a man to the esteem of his fellows. The Convention brought such men together in an aristocracy of talent and status, united by common aims and aspirations to national greatness. They represented not the people's will, but the nation's potential.[3]

If the personal experiences and concerns of the framers shaped the Preamble, their words were not fixed in meaning by that experience and those concerns when the document left their hands. Quite the contrary. Once the Preamble passed from the Convention to the public arena, other men imputed meaning to it based on their own experiences and concerns. The language refused to lie dead on the paper. Had the words been entombed in the document, they could never have remained important to a people whose experiences and society would change so drastically over time. Thus, despite some jurists' avowed fidelity to an interpretative strategy of "original meaning" or "original intent," historians know that the meanings that framers see in words and their intent in choosing words does not determine how those words will be read by later generations. "New values are invented and old ones given new content."[4]

The story of the Preamble may have begun at the Philadelphia Convention, but it did not end there. Though not questioned at the convention, the Preamble began to draw fire when the document arrived at the state ratification conventions. From the ratification conventions, through the debates on states' rights and slavery in the antebellum years, through a civil war and the Reconstruction of the nation, to the creation of new Progressive and New Deal federal agencies, and finally to the concept of a second constitution empowering rather than limiting government and guaranteeing equality, the Preamble became the centerpiece of a constitution for all the people.

What made the Preamble so remarkable was its capacity for growth over time. Revisited by new generations of constitutional thinkers and political leaders, it proved responsive to expanding perceptions of liberty and justice. The whole of the Preamble would come to undermine invidious and exclusive distinctions in the law. Its open-ended language accommodated such expansive readings.

................

"Comparisons," the great humorist Mark Twain wrote, "are odious, but they need not be malicious." No book on the Preamble can avoid comparison of it with those other superb examples of American political scripture, the Declaration of Independence and the Bill of Rights.

Like the Preamble, the Declaration was the work of a committee of five and had a single primary draftsman. While John Adams, Benjamin Franklin, Robert R. Livingston, Jr., and Roger Sherman no doubt had influence on the shape of the Declaration, the work came largely from the hand of Thomas Jefferson. The Preamble's drafting committee, including Alexander Hamilton, James Madison, Rufus King, and William Samuel Johnson, was as distinguished as its predecessor, and again assigned to one member, Gouverneur Morris, the task of rearranging the unwieldy twenty-three articles of the draft Constitution into the seven articles we now have.

Why then are the words of the Declaration a sacred text, memorized by American schoolchildren, about which "almost too much has been written" while the origin and later development of the Preamble's equally ennobling language is known to a relative handful of scholars, jurists, and bibliophiles? In part the reason lies in the history of the two texts. Jefferson's labors took nearly a month. Morris's took less than a week. The Declaration was long awaited and fully debated in the Congress. The Preamble was presented to the Convention at the eleventh hour and accepted without a murmur by the delegates. When the members of Congress adopted the Declaration they were setting out on the great journey to Independence and nationhood. When the delegates to the convention accepted the Preamble, that stage of the journey was coming to a close. By the early nineteenth century, Americans had fixed on the Declaration's opening lines as the true measure of the Revolution's highest aspirations, while in the same years the equally inspiring language of the Preamble seemed to threaten an increasingly fragile and delicate balance of power between the states and the central government.[5]

Another comparison between the two documents is warranted. On the one hand, when abolitionists sought legal grounds for ending slavery, they turned to the Declaration's Preamble, and called it law (technically they argued that the federal Constitution incorporated the Declaration). It was a brilliant but losing argument. The Constitution did not incorporate the Declaration. But its Preamble did promise the blessings of liberty and justice. The way in which that promise was negated is traced in the pages that follow. On the other hand, when Abraham Lincoln and the Republicans sought a basis for saving the Union, the Preamble to the Constitution perfectly suited their purpose.

The Bill of Rights idea was well established when the delegates gathered in Philadelphia that spring of 1787. Most states had some enumerations of rights either preceding or embedded in their state constitutions. The delegates included certain of these rights, for example a bar on ex post facto prosecutions, bills of attainder, and suspension of the writ of habeas corpus, in Article I, Section 9 of the Constitution. An effort to include a more extensive list (for example protecting free speech, press, the right of assembly, the right to a jury trial, and the right to counsel) failed after a relatively brief debate. The United States Congress supplied this want in its very first session, James Madison introducing the legislation. The final version of the Bill of Rights, a series of twelve amendments, went to the states, and ten were ratified within two years.[6]

The Bill of Rights had no Preamble, or rather, their Preamble was the Preamble to the Constitution itself, so one might have read them in light of the Preamble, but the Bill of Rights is a series of prohibitions limiting what government can do while the Preamble is a series of positive commands to government to perform its duties in the best interest of the people. Those are very different propositions.

States' bills of rights proliferated in the years before, during, and after the ratification of the ten amendments to the federal Constitution, and these often had miniature preambles of their own. These preambles justified or explained the operative portions of the amendments that followed, but did not of themselves direct government to act in any particular way. Typically, in the 1784 New Hampshire state constitution, one finds that "The Liberty of the Press is essential to the security of freedom in a state; it ought, therefore, to be inviolably preserved." The preamble stated the importance of freedom of the press, but did not require the government to do anything. Rather, government was to refrain from interfering with the press (though as events shortly proved, the publication of editorial pieces or reportage disparaging officials could be prosecuted after they appeared).[7]

. . . . . . . . . . . . . . . .

Comparisons to one side, no one should deny that the Committee of Style had written a remarkable and enduring expression of American ideals. This is their story, and ours. In the following pages, my plan has been to integrate intellectual history, legal history, and political history. I have tried to locate the debates over the clauses of the Preamble in both immediate political context and longer term constitutional theory. Some of the discourse in my sources is self-interested or even intentionally misleading. Madison warned his colleagues, a warning that is still applicable, of the dangers of self-interest and faction. Some of what they said, however, reflected an ongoing ideological debate over the shape and function of government. I have tried to see the genuineness of the latter without ignoring the time and place in which the words were said or written.

The work has a sub-theme, if that is the right term. I do not want to press it too hard, but the fact is that, with a few exceptions, the makers of our fundamental law were lawyers. While a Madison may have worked tirelessly behind the scenes, a Franklin watched paternally, and a Washington stood solemn guard, the men who did the drafting of the Declaration, the Preamble, and the Constitution were trained legal craftsmen. Throughout the revolutionary, confederation, and early national eras, lawyers wrote and interpreted republican constitutionalism. In the years that followed, lawyers like Joseph Story and Abraham Lincoln weighed the meaning of the Preamble in the scales of a union on the verge of self-destruction. In the twentieth century the legacy of the Preamble was once more hotly debated by lawyers. They asked if its promises were legally enforceable. That debate continues.

Historians too may ask if the Preamble can be made enforceable, a template for progressive government rather than a mere statement of principles. But that is not the subject for history so much as for those who we chose to govern us, and for the sovereign people who do the choosing.

# Dinner at Mrs. Dailey's Boarding House

I n the spring of 1787 Philadelphia played host to the new American nation's luminaries. A constitutional convention drew them to the elegant Georgian statehouse between Fifth and Sixth Streets on Chestnut in the heart of the city. Some of the visitors had been here before, when delegates from the thirteen colonies gathered in a Continental Congress to protest British policy. They had signed the Declaration of Independence in the assembly hall. Once again a crisis brought state legislators, judges, and governors to the city. The confederation of the United States of America was failing. Could these fifty-five men frame a new kind of federal system that would endure?

The inns and boarding houses lining Philadelphia's Market and Broad Streets eagerly welcomed the delegates. Among these establishments was the widow Mrs. Dailey's, on Third and Market. This season demand was so great that some delegates shared rooms in the city's boarding houses, but at Dailey's the delegates had each their own accommodations. Alexander Hamilton of New York, who stayed there when he attended the convention, found her business acumen impressive enough to write about it to friends.[1]

The focal point of any well-run boarding house was the victuals it offered. If Mrs. Dailey's table was typical, she set out breakfast and dinner "family style." Not elegantly prepared—cooking classes and precise measurement of ingredients for recipes were years in the future—the food was nevertheless plentiful. Eastern Pennsylvania was

9

the breadbasket of the nation. Mrs. Dailey bought from local farmers' markets. As well, Philadelphia's Delaware River port was the busiest in the nation, and its warehouses on Front Street groaned with spices and condiments from all over the world. The well-larded boarding house pantry offered its patrons pepper, cinnamon, nutmeg, cloves, horseradish, butter, jellies, jams, honey, and molasses to season foods, and pickled vegetables of all kinds. More substantial foods included eggs, waffles, donuts (a Dutch specialty, along with pancakes and cookies), fried and baked pork products, fruit pies, meat pies, game, chicken prepared in a variety of fashions, potatoes, corn, beans, and fresh caught salmon, sturgeon, trout, and catfish, as well as oysters and other shellfish, breads, biscuits, rolls, and muffins, all washed down with cider, beer, wine, tea, and coffee. Dinner was the heaviest meal of the day. Breakfast and supper, served early and late in the day, were lighter. But no one who boarded at Mrs. Dailey's went away hungry.

The eighteenth century ushered table etiquette into the boarding house. The introduction of chairs replacing the older benches and individual table settings with tableware and flatware imposed rules on the genteel and the would-be genteel diner. Most tables did not have table cloths, but the better set tables did have cloth napkins and individual eating implements. Forks were a novelty. Diners ate with spoons and the rounded edges of knives. Boarding houses were often the subject of rude jokes about the reach of the diners; visitors complained about "the total want of all the usual courtesies of the table" including "the still more frightful manner of cleaning the teeth afterwards with a pocket knife." George Washington's *Rules for Civility* (1774) included admonitions on etiquette at the table. When seated at the table, "put not your Hands to any Part of the Body, not usually Discovered"; "Being Set at meat Scratch not neither Spit Cough or blow your Nose except there's a Necessity for it"; "Put not your meat to your Mouth with your Knife in your hand neither Spit forth the Stones of any fruit Pye upon a Dish nor Cast anything under the table."[2]

The boarding house dinner table was a male preserve, and two of the regulars at Mrs. Dailey's table that spring and summer were Hamilton and Gouverneur Morris. Hamilton was born on January 11, 1755 (or 1757—the date is uncertain). "Slight and thin shouldered, with a distinctly Scottish appearance, with a florid complexion, reddish brown hair, and sparkling blue eyes" he was an attractive addition to the dinner table. Orphaned early, his youth was one of poverty but his almost sur-real determination to improve himself, his quick and sure grasp of facts and ideas, his capacity for loyalty, and his personal courage had en-deared him to a succession of mentors on the island of Nevis in the West Indies, in New Jersey, to which he migrated as a youth of fifteen, and in New York City, where he matriculated at King's College in 1773. In the first days of the armed conflict between the patriots and the British he joined a company of volunteers and later they elected him their captain. His service in the cause between 1776 and 1777 brought him to George Washington's notice, and Washington selected him as an aide-de-camp and elevated him to a lieutenant-colonelcy. A war hero, he married well (into the powerful New York Schuyler clan). He served in the Continental Congress in 1782 and 1783. It took him but six months of reading (with help from James Duane, a lawyer and col-league in the Schuyler circle) to satisfy the New York bar examination committee, and soon he had established a thriving practice. "Touchy" and sometimes violently combative, "he never outgrew the stigma of his illegitimacy," but he was much loved by his friends and had great capacity for friendship himself. A career of merit and partisanship as a member of the first federal administration and later as the leader of the Federalist Party was ended by his New York political rival, Aaron Burr in 1804. A bullet from Burr's dueling pistol entered Hamilton's spine, and he died, in agony, a little over a day later.[3]

Gouverneur Morris was Hamilton's friend to the end. A little over six feet tall, broad of shoulder and hip, with a large well formed head atop a solid neck, his appetite for food and other creature com-forts was already the talk of the town. Well known for his convivial manners, his many speculative financial arrangements, and his flirta-tious way with the ladies, he surely was a center of attention at Mrs. Dailey's as well as at the sessions of the Constitutional Convention.

Morris was born on January 31, 1752, on his father's vast Mor-risiana Hudson River estate. His family was wealthy, owning ex-tensive lands on the east bank of the Hudson, in what is now the New York City borough of the Bronx. He was "quite literally, to the manor born." But the political loyalties of his family divided it dur-ing the Revolution—his father and older brother remaining loyal to the crown while Gouverneur distinguished himself as a patriot. He went to King's College (renamed Columbia after the Revolution) at age twelve in 1764, graduated in 1768, and received a master's degree

Gouverneur Morris Esq'r., member of congress, by Pierre Eugène Du Simitière, 1783.
*Courtesy of the Library of Congress, LC-USZ62-45482.*

in 1771. A lawyer by training and trade, he was also a veteran politician and would after the convention become a diplomat, serving the United States as its minister to France. He died in 1816 on the very estate where he was born, his passing reported to the nation by his long time friend Rufus King.[4]

Morris's interest in politics began in 1775, when he was elected from his family's district to the colony's Provincial Congress, a revolutionary body. He then represented New York at the Continental Congress. His service on its military affairs committee taught him the importance of a strong national government and the weakness of the confederation. In 1779, he relocated to Philadelphia and there opened a law office. In 1780, an accident with a runaway carriage cost him his leg below the knee, but not his zest for life or his career in politics. His next office, from 1781 to 1785, brought him back to the Congress, this time representing Pennsylvania, and from 1782 to 1785 he served as an assistant to Robert Morris in the Office of Finance. The shambles of the confederation's finances—debt, a worthless currency, all sorts of corruption—did not deter him from investing on his own account. He had "something of the Midas touch in business," avoiding the ill-fated speculative schemes that later landed Robert Morris in debtor's prison.[5]

Historians have described Gouverneur Morris as "all flamboyance and talent...happy to share his opinions on any subject, Morris suffered fools not at all." But he could be "defiant and inflammatory in defense" of his views, offending other delegates with his "belligerence." Away from politics, he was much sought after at social events. "The 'Tall Boy' was as much a hedonist as an intellectual." He scandalized the convention's proper New Englanders by his open "philandering." But no one could doubt that the "brilliant and urbane" lawyer-turned-statesman was a force to be reckoned with.[6]

Meals at boarding houses were occasions for conversation. Morris and Hamilton would have dominated these exchanges at Mrs. Dailey's. Hamilton could be a charming conversationalist, and the "tall boy" could talk up a storm. According to James Madison's notes, Morris spoke more often at the convention than any other delegate (with characteristic modesty, Madison did not add "other than myself"). He no doubt carried that delight in hearing his own voice to the table. But the rules adopted when the convention was called to order forbade the delegates revealing what transpired in the statehouse. Morris would have chaffed at these, so wedded was he to airing his views. Still, as Madison later recalled, at the table Morris was the most genial of companions. Morris was capable of "a candid surrender of his opinions when the lights of discussion satisfied him that they had been too hastily formed, and a readiness to aid in making the best of measures in which he had been overruled." In any case, Morris no doubt found other subjects of conversation to pass the time.[7]

On the evening of September 8, 1787, Hamilton and Morris had no time to waste on table talk. The convention had tapped the two men along with Madison, Rufus King, and William Samuel Johnson to serve as a Committee of Style and Arrangement. Their task was daunting—to revise the document the delegates had drafted. It had an unwieldy shape, twenty-three articles defining the duties of various branches of the proposed federal government, its relation to the state governments, and its manner of proceeding.

The committee had asked Morris to prepare a first draft of the revision. The opening lines of the document he was given immediately drew his attention. More a preface than a preamble, it had passed through the stages of debate and revision of the following articles largely unchanged because it was thought unimportant. It now read "We the people of the states of New-Hampshire, Massachusetts, Rhode-Island and Providence Plantations, Connecticut, New-York, New-Jersey, Pennsylvania, Delaware, Maryland, Virginia, North-Carolina, South-Carolina, and Georgia, do ordain, declare and establish the following constitution for the government of ourselves and our posterity"—in short, the preamble to a union of states. Morris had seen it in the printed draft constitution the Committee of Detail circulated a month earlier. He wondered, could he get away with changing it to make it fit his own very different ideas of Union and of the higher purposes of government?

Five days later, on September 12, 1787, the committee reported its revisions to the convention. No doubt the other members had all made contributions to the final document, but Morris was its principal draftsman. The Preamble was the jewel in this crowning achievement. The language of its provisions was not entirely original, but where it differed from the language given Morris, it set the new nation on a course far different from a confederation.

................

This was not the first time Morris had thought long and hard about the nature of union and the purposes of government. Only twenty-five miles northwest of where he sat at Mrs. Dailey's dinner table on Market Street lay the detritus of the revolutionary army camp at Valley Forge. In the winter of 1777–1778, a younger, thinner, and far hungrier Morris decided that the Continental Congress was a failure. Something must be done to change that situation.

# CHAPTER 1

.........................

# The Revolutionary Republics, the Confederation, and Their Laws

Before the Revolutionary War Valley Forge, Pennsylvania, "was a rural village, about two thousand acres of wooded hill dotted by occasional clearing, surrounding farmhouses, and outlying buildings." The valley was part of the rich agricultural landscape of the middle colonies, its wheat and hogs went to Philadelphia mills and slaughterhouses, there baked into bread and cured into bacon, and sent to the British West Indies to feed the slaves working on the sugar plantations.[1]

Today Valley Forge National Park is almost prissily clean. Although guides in period costumes lead groups of tourists along the twisting paths between the huts of a long lost Continental Army camp, it is hard to imagine what conditions were like for that army. A welcome center is filled with chintzy Revolutionary War souvenirs, and one can book a wedding or other affair through the park's convention website. In the summer, the landscape is lush, a refuge from the heavily trafficked highways leading into Philadelphia. In winter, however, the twisty narrow roads become treacherous, and radio reports every fifteen minutes in morning and evening inform motorists that traffic on Route 23 is once again snarled by an accident or two. It is winter's icy grip that reminds us of the Valley Forge of 1777–1778.

On January 21, 1778, twenty-five-year-old Gouverneur Morris arrived in York, Pennsylvania. He found the Second Continental Congress hastily setting up shop after being chased out of Philadelphia. British troops occupied the town. He too was on the run. A lawyer with a growing practice in New York City he could no longer

Valley Forge, 1777. *Gen. Washington and Lafayette visiting the suffering part of the army,* by A. Gibert (artist) and P. Haas (lithographer). *Courtesy of the Library of Congress, LC-USZ62-819.*

exploit (the British occupied the city), a bon vivant who now could enjoy few occasions of elegant entertainment, he found himself the newly chosen delegate from his state to attend the ineffectual and often stultifying sessions of the Congress. The state's provisional convention, itself moving about the Hudson Valley one step ahead of General Sir Henry Clinton's army, had some months earlier pasted together a constitution in whose drafting Morris had taken some part. Much respected by his peers in the state's provisional legislature (after all, he was a Morris, and the Morrises owned a good part of the eastern shore of the Hudson), Morris had been sent off by them to find the Continental Congress.[2]

The very same day on which he presented his credentials to the Congress, the Committee on Military Affairs took a moment away from drafting and posting messages to its generals and sent Morris off to report on the condition of Commander-in-Chief George Washington's troops. The Continental Army was quartered at Valley Forge. There, Washington was as near despair as his remarkable self-possession would let him betray. On December 27, 1777, he had written to Congress, "I am now convinced, beyond a doubt that unless some great and capital change suddenly takes place in that line, this Army must inevitably be reduced to one or other of these three things. Starve, dissolve, or disperse, in order to obtain subsistence in the best manner they can." The men were eating anything to fill their bellies. Washington pleaded, "This is not an exaggerated picture, but [and] that I have abundant reason to support what I say." It was this letter, on top of his other similar laments, that convinced Congress to send a fresh set of eyes to confirm the general's assessment.[3]

Morris met Washington, toured the facility, and could hardly believe his senses. The cold could not suppress the fetid odor of sickness nor did the snow conceal the ragged clothing of the troops. Two weeks later, Morris wrote a letter to John Jay, a fellow New York lawyer and friend. Valley Forge had opened his eyes to an appalling sight. "The skeleton of an army presents itself to our eyes in a naked, starving, condition, out of health, out of spirits." The camp reeked of corruption. Corruption emanating from the British crown had been one reason the Revolutionaries gave for terminating the relationship with the home country. At the start of the war, the American troops boasted that there was no corruption in their ranks because their cause was national. That patriotism had now faded. The "rage militaire" of the first years had given way to cynicism throughout the ranks. Many soldiers were punished for fighting with one another, disobeying their officers, and even deserting. The army's quartermasters made deals on the side and lined their pockets. "The free, open, and undisturbed communication with the city of Philadelphia, debauches the minds of those in its vicinage, with astonishing rapidity. This State [of Pennsylvania] is sick even unto the death."[4]

Though he did not hide his shock, Morris was optimistic that better management might make a difference to the men's condition. As early as 1775 he had drafted notes to himself on how to finance the protest. Now he was sharing them with Jay. "Congress have sent me to this place, in conjunction with some other gentlemen, to regulate their army, and in truth not a little regulation has become necessary." Unlike Washington, it was not only the morale of the troops that worried Morris. Instead, Morris saw that problem in fiscal terms. More government spending, wisely applied, would save the army. "The mighty Senate of America is not what you have known it. The Continental Congress and currency have both depreciated, but, in the hands of the Almighty architect of empires, the stone, which the builders have rejected, may easily become head of the corner[stone]" of the capitol of a great empire called the United States.

Something must be done to make a great nation out of a pitiful coalition of states barely able to wage a war necessary for their own survival. Something must be done, but what? The war hung in the scales; the great experiment in Independence balanced against the incompetence of the Congress. In the midst of an armed camp of starving farmers waging war against their former imperial master, a shivering young lawyer from one of the colonies' richest families dreamed of a great republic founded on good laws.

## The Lawyers' Revolution

Morris may have seemed out of place as a lawyer in a military camp, but nothing could have been more appropriate for the future of American constitutionalism. For the story of the American Revolution and the story of the drafting of the Preamble to the federal Constitution are inseparably interwoven. The words and phrases, the ideas and ideals, that would announce the determination of the American people to be free of their imperial bonds, and the clauses of the Preamble that would bind a nation together under one frame of government, were the work of one and the same cadre of revolutionary lawyers. Morris was one of the youngest of these, along with his good friends John Jay and Rufus King. Others included John Adams, John Dickinson, Patrick Henry, Thomas Jefferson, and James Wilson. Together they labored to turn laws for the colonies of a distant empire into laws for a sovereign people. As the revolutionaries cast off imperial authority the patriot lawyers provided brilliant legal reasons to depose royal governors, dismiss chartered assemblies, and dispossess thousands of men and women who remained loyal to the king.[5]

How could the patriot lawyers not be part of the movement to restore the rights of Englishmen to the American shore? Rights were the essence of legal argument for resistance and later for independence. The revolutionary case for rights was simply a macrocosm of what lawyers did in their everyday occupation, zealous advocacy, only this time their client was the American people.

Seen from the lawyers' point of view, what transpired in the years between 1763 and 1776 was an ongoing argument about the role of "the people" in their own governance. With so many of their countrymen (compared to the English electorate) able to vote in local and colony-wide elections, the colonial lawyers came to believe that the exercise of power must represent the will of the people. Their English counterparts, used to a House of Commons elected by a relative handful of propertied men and badly apportioned (London sent fewer men to the House of Commons than a handful of medieval boroughs whose voters could be counted in double digits), believed that the people could be represented "virtually." Virtual representation meant that members of Parliament could vote on the basis of their own understanding of the people's best interest, rather than following the instructions of the people who elected them. This idea English authorities extended to the colonies, whose voters sent no one to Parliament. No one had a right to instruct a member of Parliament against his better judgment.

At the heart of the notion of right of self-government which the Americans advocated was that the real rulers must be we the people. This notion was framed by seventeenth-century English republican writers like Algernon Sidney, James Harrington, and finally John Locke. They insisted that government was instituted to protect the rights of the people, and the people had the right to remove a government that violated this precept. But even as Locke (anonymously) published his *Two Treatises on Government* in 1690, Lockean notions of a government whose officers were servants of the people bound by fundamental law were being overwritten by parliamentary politicians and placemen.

Locke's ideas about popular sovereignty found a home in the colonies, along with the writings of many other critics of absolute parliamentary power. When these English political reformers railed against the corruption of Parliament by greedy ministers of the crown and greedier private interests, American lawyers were listening. In the protests that erupted after the close of the French and Indian War, in 1763, the outlines of a colossal plot against the people's liberty in England became clear to the revolutionary lawyers. But how to frame legal protests against the overweening power of a corrupt Parliament when the ultimate source of legal authority was Parliament? This was the challenge for the patriot lawyers.[6]

In 1768, James Wilson wrote but did not publish his thoughts on opposition to parliamentary enactments. Born in Scotland in 1742, he followed a good number of his countrymen in seeking new opportunities in the colonies. He had trained at Scottish colleges, and when he arrived in Philadelphia in 1766 he gained employment as a teacher at the College of Philadelphia (later renamed the University of Pennsylvania). He also read law in John Dickinson's office, becoming one of the most learned, if not the most wealthy, of that distinguished revolutionary cadre. He voted for independence and served briefly as an officer in the new state's militia. Named to the Constitutional Convention, he was a leading light there and at the Pennsylvania state ratification convention that followed. He was one of the first justices of the United States Supreme Court, a lecturer in law at the University of Pennsylvania, and a leading expert on the Constitution. He died in office, in 1798, while on judicial circuit in North Carolina, his highly meritorious public career marred by his speculation in western lands and his imprisonment on two occasions for not paying his creditors what he owed.[7]

Wilson was a brilliant legal thinker, and took the first giant step away from English legal precedents for resistance and toward what would become government based on the sovereignty of the people. He asked himself, "On what principles, then, on what motives of action, can we depend for the security of our liberties, of our properties...of life itself?" Not Parliament, surely, for Parliament was riven with corruption. Wilson concluded that "it is repugnant to the essential maxims of jurisprudence, to the ultimate end of all governments, to the genius of the British constitution, and to the liberty and happiness of the colonies, that they should be bound by the legislative authority of Great Britain." But did not the "British constitution" make Parliament supreme? It did.[8]

Where then arose the rightful authority for the governance of Americans? Wilson at first regarded himself as an Anglo-American lawyer arguing within the framework of a British Empire and its laws. But to overcome the obstacle of the supremacy of Parliament, Wilson proposed that Americans see the charters and grants that inaugurated the colonies in a new light. Instead of mere privileges granted by the king and regulated by Parliament, he recast the colonial assemblies as repositories of the people's will. Against a Parliament whose majority was increasingly indifferent to American claims of right, Wilson set the colonial governments as resting on the consent of the governed. Other revolutionary lawyers followed his lead.[9]

Between 1774 and 1775, the patriot lawyers fashioned a law based on rights that existed in nature rather than privileges granted by governments. At the core of those rights was government by the people. As Wilson told the Pennsylvania Provincial Assembly in 1774, there had been "a great compact between the king and his people," which king and Parliament violated when they took away self-government from Massachusetts in 1774. The abridgment of charter provisions for election of legislators there breached the tie of allegiance of colonists to the empire. "All attempts to alter the charter or constitution of [a] colony, unless by the authority of its own legislature, are violations of its rights, and illegal." Wilson had transmuted royal charters into "constitutions" preceding and enabling government that limited the power of their royal grantor. The people should have the liberty to frame their own governments.[10]

## A Declaration of the People

The Declaration of Independence rested upon the patriot lawyers' argument for the sovereignty of the people. While the Second Continental Congress waited for Virginia's Richard Henry Lee to return from the Virginia Provincial Congress with a formal proposal for independence, five delegates who favored that step were asked to prepare a declaration explaining the reasons why the colonies should be independent.

Of that committee, John Adams, Roger Sherman, Robert R. Livingston Jr., and Thomas Jefferson all were lawyers with busy legal practices. The only member of the committee not a lawyer, Benjamin Franklin, had already reached the conclusion that independence must be declared. He had earlier hoped for promotion within the imperial system, perhaps even the governorship of Pennsylvania if the crown took the proprietorship of the colony away from the Penn family. But in 1774, that door to preferment closed when Franklin was discovered to have leaked former governor Thomas Hutchinson's private correspondence to the Massachusetts patriots. Franklin returned home to Philadelphia a disillusioned and angry man, and would very shortly become outspoken in his patriot views. He helped polemicist Thomas Paine to find employment and to publish his blast at the crown. Chosen as a delegate to the Continental Congresses, Franklin was an early advocate of independence. But his part in the committee's work was not without sadness, for as it met, Benjamin's loyalist son William Franklin, royal governor of New Jersey, was jailed by a revolutionary tribunal.[11]

Franklin was joined on the committee to draft a declaration by John Adams. Stiff, sometimes self-righteous, full of ideas, fiercely pro-New England, Adams had advocated greater independence for the colonies for the previous decade. With his cousin Samuel Adams, John lobbied his fellow delegates for a declaration of independence. Adams had a "combustible temper" directed at those who did not understand the gravity of the crisis or the need for quick action. Indeed, his words were more eloquent than his appearance, for "at thirty-nine, Adams had already lost much of his hair, several of his teeth, and any semblance of a waistline."[12]

For his part, Adams did not find fellow committee member Roger Sherman of Connecticut a particularly attractive public speaker. "Sherman's air is the reverse of grace. There cannot be a more striking contrast to beautiful action, than the motions of his hands. Generally, he stands upright with his hands before him. The fingers of his left hand clenched into a fist, and the wrist of it, grasped with his right hand…when he moves a hand, in anything like action, [the English illustrator William] Hogarth's genius could not have invented as motion more opposite to grace. It is stiffness, and awkwardness, itself. Rigid as starched linen or buckram." But Sherman was more than a simple cobbler from Connecticut. He was a largely self-taught "distinguished jurist and political leader" who would take his place at both the Continental Congress and the Philadelphia Constitutional Convention. Adams respected his toughmindedness and political sagacity, as well he should, for Sherman had a hand in just about every project that turned the thirteen colonies into a great nation.[13]

The fourth member of the committee came from one of the foremost clans in the colonies, the Livingstons of New York. Robert R. Livingston Jr. (known to history as "the chancellor" to distinguish him others in his clan, Robert being such a common family name that biographers sometimes get the various Robert Livingstons confused) was a lawyer and landowner who very reluctantly contemplated independence. But he sided with the Whig or patriot faction and was a staunch supporter of the war effort. Known for his judicial temper, he would become the first chancellor of the state of New York and later the diplomat who helped negotiate the Louisiana Purchase in 1803.[14]

The committee turned to its fifth member, Thomas Jefferson of Virginia, to prepare a first draft of the Declaration. Jefferson was courteous in public and sharp tongued in private, a veritable mass of contradictions. Thirty-three years old when he drafted the Declaration, he came from the same circle as Randolph and the other great families of Virginia, but he was never a friend to the idea of aristocracy. A man who wrote warmly of Enlightenment rationality and who foresaw a world freed of the superstition of priests and the tyranny of despots, he never quite freed himself from the shackles of a world of rank and privilege. His idea of equality, for example, did not extend to slaves, of whom he owned many and freed only a few, or women, whom he thought belonged "in the peaceful sphere of domestic tranquility," a view blissfully ignorant of the hardships of bearing children, maintaining a household, tending the sick, and the drudgery of family care every woman endured.[15]

No figure among the founding fathers is as controversial as Jefferson. Raised to the highest honors his countrymen could bestow— governor of Virginia, minister to France, Secretary of State, vice president and then president of the United States for two terms— no man of such disinterested civic service was ever so reviled in his lifetime as Jefferson. Historians' views of him are similarly disparate; he is either beloved or despised. In fine, he is the essential "American Sphinx…the enigmatic and elusive touchstone for the most cherished convictions and contested truths in American culture." But this fact about Jefferson cannot be gainsaid. "Jefferson was virtually unique in the strength and passion of his commitment to one crowning ideal: that this revolution was universal…the forerunner of an age of democratic revolution."[16]

Jefferson was the obvious choice as principal draftsman. His "Summary View of the Rights of British America" in 1774 paralleled Wilson's thinking in elegant prose. Americans' rights derived from their unaided efforts to establish settlements in the wilderness, not from privileges the crown deigned to allow. Jefferson's "Declaration of the Necessity of the Causes of Taking Up Arms" of 1775 was a masterwork, bringing together political realities and high-minded political theory. In it, he wrote, "a reverence for our Creator, principles of humanity, and the dictates of common sense, must convince all those who reflect upon the subject, that government was instituted to promote the welfare of mankind, and ought to be administered for the attainment of that end." When crown and Parliament conspired to impose on Americans a tyranny unfitted to their native love of freedom, the Americans protested. "We saw the misery to which such despotism would reduce us. We for ten years incessantly and ineffectually besieged the throne as supplicants; we reasoned, we remonstrated with parliament, in the most mild and decent language." The only recourse was armed resistance. "Honour, justice, and humanity, forbid us tamely to surrender that freedom which we received from our gallant ancestors, and which our innocent posterity have a right to receive from us. We cannot endure the infamy and guilt of resigning succeeding generations to that wretchedness which inevitably awaits them, if we basely entail hereditary bondage upon them. Our cause is just. Our union is perfect. Our internal resources are great, and, if necessary, foreign assistance is undoubtedly attainable."[17]

Jefferson had written, "our union is perfect," as if one people had spoken in protest; as if all the people thought as one. "Our union is perfect" was hardly a true statement (there were as many Americans loyal to the crown in 1776 as there were revolutionaries), but it was an ideal captured in a stroke of stylistic brilliance that would motivate Congress, a year later, to ask the committee of five to explain and justify independence, and that committee to entrust the task to Jefferson.

Working by daylight and candlelight through the final weeks of June, 1776, Jefferson labored to produce the Declaration. Never a particularly able public speaker, he filled his handwritten draft of the document with diacritical marks to help him read it to the Congress when the committee deemed it ready. But he understood in a profound way that the document must speak in the grandest terms. As such, it needed a preamble, and that preamble must be the voice of one people.[18]

Although the opening lines of the Declaration are now an immortal memorial to the aspirations of the revolutionaries, Jefferson did not write on their behalf, or on the behalf of the states, or even the Continental Congress. Instead, he began, "When in the course of human events, it becomes necessary for one people to dissolve the political bands which have connected them with another, and to assume among the powers of the earth, the separate and equal station to which the laws of nature and of nature's God entitle them, a decent respect to the opinions of mankind requires that they should declare the causes which impel them to the separation." Again he spoke for "one people." This salutation was no accident. He had long seen the protest as a people's movement. As he later recalled of the events leading to his election to the Congress, "The people met generally, with anxiety & alarm in their countenances, and the effect of the day thro' the whole colony was like a shock of electricity, arousing every man & placing him erect & solidly on his centre. They universally chose delegates for the convention." "Every man" was (allowing for the special circumstances of citizenship in Virginia) equivalent to "We the People."[19]

In the end, although the thoughts of the founders were, as Jefferson wrote to Adams, little more than "a great experiment in liberty," the basis of revolutionary self-government was now "We the People." Jefferson confided to Edward Carrington in 1785, "I am persuaded myself that the good sense of the people will always be found to be the best army. They may be led astray for a moment, but will soon correct themselves. The people are the only censors of their governors: and even their errors will tend to keep these to the true principles of their institution." But when he wrote these words, Jefferson was on a diplomatic mission in France, far from the mounting troubles that faced the new United States of America.[20]

## State Constitutions

Jefferson supplied a draft of a constitution to the committee charged with the task of writing one for Virginia. Rhode Island and Connecticut recast their old charters as constitutions. The other states' provisional governments set about writing or calling a convention to write constitutions. Under revolutionary republican ideology, a constitution was the fundamental law of the new state, conferring authority on the government to operate in the name of the sovereign people.

But not all the people were included in political community of the new states, as the constitution of Virginia demonstrated. George

Mason was the author of the Virginia Constitution. In 1776, Mason was thirty-nine years old, already ridden with painful gout, and the recently widowed father of twelve children. A planter largely self-taught, and the owner of a considerable number of slaves, he nevertheless abhorred slavery in the abstract (as did Jefferson). The two men were in constant correspondence that spring and early summer, and Jefferson's suggestions were as important to Mason as Mason's draft of a Virginia Bill of Rights was to Jefferson. The Declaration of Independence's opening phrases would frame the preamble to the state constitution, but the latter amended the Declaration to add the words "When in a state of society." At a stroke of the pen, slaves, a large minority of Virginia's population, were left out of the polity. The new constitution's preamble continued that the people (less its bondsmen) "do ordain and declare the future form of government of Virginia to be as follows." The phrase "ordain and declare" modified to "ordain and establish" would soon see further use.[21]

Drafters of other state constitutions merged the one-people concept of independence with some form of republican representative self-government. The formula for representation varied from state to state. The revolutionaries debated the basis for drawing electoral districts—too large and the representative would not know who he represented, too small and local prejudices outweighed the common good—but in general, states opted for small districts, sometimes no larger than a single township or county. In most of the states, the preference for small districts gave wealthier, better established eastern regions more seats in the legislature than poorer, more dispersed western people.

There were differences of opinion as well over whether the colonial practice of requiring voters to possess property or pay a certain amount of taxes to qualify for voting should be continued, or whether all free white Protestant males should have the franchise. During a controversy over the same proposal in Maryland, one anti-property pamphleteer railed, "it would be unjust and oppressive in the extreme to shut out the poor in having a share in declaring who shall be the lawgivers of their country, and yet [they] bear a very heavy share in the support of government." Maryland retained its property-holding qualification for voting. Pennsylvania gave the vote to all males who paid taxes and believed in the divine inspiration of the Old and New Testaments. The odd pairing of religious liberty and religious establishmentarianism reappeared in the state's Declaration of Rights. "All men have a natural and unalienable right to worship Almighty God according to the dictates of their own consciences and understanding" the constitution proclaimed, and "no man ought or of right can be compelled to attend any religious worship, or erect or support any place of worship, or maintain any ministry, contrary to, or against, his own free will and consent." But only the man "who acknowledges the being of a God" had the full panoply of rights of citizenship. Religious qualifications for voting and holding office prevailed in almost all of the other new states.[22]

Instead of the multiple officeholding and overlapping executive, legislative, and judicial functions that Britain's ministers of state, members of Parliament, and colonial governors performed, states adopted a system of checks and balances. In the latter, three distinct branches of government—a bi-cameral (two house) legislature, an executive, and a judiciary—would have the means to prevent one another from gaining too much power. Pennsylvania's and Georgia's first constitutions featured unicameral legislatures. Vermont, at this time a separate republic negotiating its future with both the British and the Continental authorities, also opted for a unicameral legislature.

The state constitutions sometimes had preambles. These stated the purposes of government and the relation of the branches of government to these purposes. They were different from the preambles commonly introducing ordinary pieces of legislation in that they had a general purpose rather than a specific one. Moreover, they spoke in terms of political philosophy rather than strict law. Many were framed as lists of rights. For example, Maryland's Constitution of 1776 began with a recital of the rights of the people, and popular sovereignty led the procession: "That all government of right originates from the people, is founded in compact only, and instituted solely for the good of the whole." North Carolina's, a few months later, proclaimed "That all political power is vested in and derived from the people only." Pennsylvania's was more extensive: "WHEREAS all government ought to be instituted and supported for the security and protection of the community as such, and to enable the individuals who compose it to enjoy their natural rights, and the other blessings which the Author of existence has bestowed upon man; and whenever these great ends of government are not obtained, the people have a right, by common consent to change it, and take such measures as to them may appear necessary to promote their safety and happiness."

James Madison, Rufus King, and Gouverneur Morris all played roles in their state's constitutional framing exercises. Madison was born on March 16, 1751, one of ten children of the wealthiest planter in Orange County, Virginia. He completed his studies at the College of New Jersey (later Princeton) in 1771. An avid reader and deep thinker even then, he was "at loose ends" when the revolutionary crisis burst upon the colonies. He had as yet little interest in politics and chose the patriot cause relatively late in the day, joining the Orange County Committee of Safety in December 1774. In the spring of 1776 he was elected to the colony's provincial congress (the royal governor had dissolved the House of Burgesses and fled to a British man-of-war off the coast) but did not contribute much to the debates over a state constitution. He did have a genuine interest in religious freedom, however, and on the floor of the assembly he persuaded George Mason, a leading figure in the congress, to replace the phrase "all men should enjoy the fullest toleration in the exercise of religion" with "all men are equally entitled to the full and free exercise of" it in a draft of the future state's bill of rights.[23]

Rufus King was born on March 24, 1755, at Scarborough, then a part of Massachusetts but now in the state of Maine. He was a son of a prosperous farmer-merchant, a supporter of the crown, and he saw his father become a target of the anti-Stamp Act mobs. Rufus's father became a loyalist, but his brothers would become stalwart supporters of the new nation. King graduated Harvard College in 1777, read the law for a year, and then volunteered for militia duty in the Revolutionary War. He served as an aide to General James Sullivan, a Maine landholder, and after his year's enlistment was completed, King returned to his legal studies and was admitted to the bar in 1780. He began a legal practice in Newburyport, Massachusetts, and was shortly thereafter elected a representative to the Massachusetts General Court (the state's lower house). Colleagues later admired his "sweet voice," reserved demeanor, and great oratorical abilities. Though still a young man, he was marked for great things.[24]

In the vanguard of protest, Massachusetts found itself lagging behind the other new states in framing a constitution acceptable to its citizens. The towns, sent the first version by the legislature in 1776, refused to ratify by a four-to-one margin. One objection was the absence of a special convention to write the constitution. Chagrined, the legislators arranged for the election of a special convention, an innovation in constitution making that would be a model for the Philadelphia Convention of 1787. The convention chose a committee of thirty to revise the draft, and the committee named James Bowdoin, Samuel Adams, and his cousin John Adams to write an improved version. John was its draftsman, a role he had declined when the Continental Congress wanted a Declaration of Independence. But he was ready this time, having fully explored the matter in his 1776 *Thoughts on Government.*

While the committee was busy at its work, King regularly attended the Newburyport town meetings. He was there when the Adams draft arrived. The meeting discussed every part of the document and then voted its "return," a provisional "yes." With the new draft in danger of failing to gain the necessary two-thirds of the towns' support, the convention declared the constitution adopted by adding the towns that ratified conditionally (upon the amendment of the document) to the towns that ratified unconditionally. The same process—vote yes now, and we will promise to amend later—would be urged by the federalists of 1787 on the state ratifying conventions.[25]

The Massachusetts Constitution of 1780 opened with a Preamble:

> PREAMBLE: The end of the institution, maintenance, and administration of government is to secure the existence of the body-politic, to protect it, and to furnish the individuals who compose it with the power of enjoying, in safety and tranquillity, their natural rights and the blessings of life; and whenever these great objects are not obtained the people have a right to alter the government, and to take measures necessary for their safety, prosperity, and happiness. The body politic is formed by a voluntary association of individuals; it is a social compact by which the whole people covenants with each citizen and each citizen with the whole people that all shall be governed by certain laws for the common good. It is the duty of the people, therefore, in framing a constitution of government, to provide for an equitable mode of making laws, as well as for an impartial interpretation and a

faithful execution of them; that every man may, at all times, find his security in them."

The preamble assumed that good government must promote tranquility and provide for the common good, values that suffused Adams' *Thoughts on Government* four years earlier.[26]

In the meantime, Massachusetts named King as one of its delegates to the Congress, a task he relished only a little less than the imbroglio in his native state. He took his seat on December 6, 1784, and discovered that he had been named to a committee to negotiate the secession of state land claims to the confederation as a national domain. Thereafter followed his appointment as a commissioner to settle the dispute between New York and New Hampshire over their respective borders (a dispute complicated by the presence of Vermont between them). While this tussle continued, the general question of the settlement of lands proceeded, and King moved, on March 16, 1785, that "after the year 1800 of the Christian era there shall be neither slavery nor involuntary servitude in any of the said States (to be carved out of the western territory) otherwise than in punishment of crimes, whereof the party shall have been convicted to have been personally guilty." It was a stance he would maintain until his death in 1827.[27]

Gouverneur Morris had a direct hand in the framing of the New York State Constitution, a process almost as contentious as Massachusetts'. In danger of capture by royal troops quartered in New York City, the provincial state government moved up the Hudson River, candid in its members' dismay that "the many tyrannical and oppressive usurpations of the King and Parliament of Great Britain on the rights and liberties of the people of the American colonies had reduced them to the necessity of introducing a government by congresses and committees, as temporary expedients." Reassembled at the village of Kingston on April 20, 1777, they displayed a nervous republicanism—for "doubts have arisen whether this [provincial] congress are invested with sufficient power and authority to deliberate and determine on so important a subject as the necessity of erecting and constituting a new form of government and internal police, to the exclusion of all foreign jurisdiction, dominion, and control whatever."[28]

But, instructed by the Congress to get down to the business of writing a constitution, Morris and the other members set aside any qualms and agreed that "it appertains of right solely to the people of this colony to determine the said doubts." After repeating the entire Declaration of Independence, the draft constitution announced that "all power whatever…hath reverted to the people thereof, and this convention hath by their suffrages and free choice been appointed, and among other things authorized to institute and establish such a government as they shall deem best calculated to secure the rights and liberties of the good people of this State, most conducive of the happiness and safety of their constituents in particular, and of America in general." The frame of government that followed, a bicameral legislature, a governor and a supreme court, exhibited the checks and balances system that Adams advocated for Massachusetts. Voting would be by ballot instead of by voice, reducing the danger of influence peddling, and a census would determine the seats in the lower house. When they got around to writing it, the constitution was a sound one. Morris later wrote that John Jay was largely responsible for the document. Jay and Morris were friends, allies, and lawyers who had represented the same clients, and they respected one another.[29]

As searing an experience for him as Valley Forge might have been, Morris was more deeply angered by the incapacity of the confederation he served. Indeed, all five of the future members of the Committee of Style had seen at first hand the confederation's weakness and came to believe that something must be done to reform its laws. The fate of the nation, and of all their sacrifices thus far to establish it, hung in the balance. Could "We the People" become more than a rhetorical flourish? Could "We the People" actually become a nation, bound together by fundamental law?

## The Perils of Independence

The transformation from colonies of a distant imperial power to self-governing republics was a remarkable feat, but the United States of America created in 1776 was anything but united. States made economic war on one another, and factions within states did battle over taxes, land titles, and voting rights. Perhaps this should not have been a surprise, for the nation was born in upheaval, a civil war of patriots against loyalists as well as a war for independence and a revolution in the structure of governance. During the war in the Carolinas, Georgia, Delaware, New Jersey, and New York, bands of loyalist guerillas and patriot militias chased one another over the countryside leaving in their wake destroyed homes, dead livestock, and burned crops. Aftershocks of that upheaval continued even after the Peace of Paris with Britain was signed in 1782 and ratified the next year. On the western and southern borders of the new nation, Indians and settlers continued a war of each against all. Both sides of the Ohio River were dark and bloody ground. In the Southeast, long a cockpit of conflict between English-speaking settlers and Muskogee Indians, there had never been any peace. A war with the United States' former ally Spain threatened along the Florida border.

The states faced indebtedness caused by the war. Some states confiscated loyalists' property and sold it at auction, while other states passed bond issues or raised taxes to pay for their soldiers' ordnance, food, and wages. Creditors and debtors in the states vied for control of the government. Speculators who bought up the securities states had issued to finance the war demanded that the securities be repaid on time at face value. By 1787, the southern states had been able to pay off these debts, but in northern states the debts were still unredeemed.

Accustomed to spending nearly half their income on imported consumer goods before the war and tired of scrimping during the fighting, Americans indulged in a buying spree after 1783. At first, British merchants offered easy credit terms, but by 1784, with exports (particularly to the Sugar Islands) lagging far behind imports, Americans could no longer pay even a part of what they owed. The flow of investment capital from Europe had dried up as well, making it harder for Americans to replace property destroyed in the war. A depression resulted that lasted until the end of the decade. Businesses failed as merchants and shopkeepers could not pay for what they had imported. Goods sat on shelves as wages in the cities fell 25 percent.[30]

The same pressures for land in the West that led to conflict with Britain pitted settlers, land development companies, and even states against one another during and after the Revolution. Congress could not contain the veterans' demand for homesteads in the Ohio Valley and the rich bottom lands of the interior Southeast. Land speculators and land companies wanted the West opened up immediately, but Indians had prior claims. In treaties at Fort Stanwix and Fort

McIntosh with New York and Ohio Indians, signed in 1784 and 1785, Congress opened the way to settlement of the eastern Ohio Valley, but the British and their Indian allies blocked further advance into the Northwest. In the meantime, settlers began to carve out farms in what would become Kentucky, Tennessee, and Alabama, sometimes without gaining title to the land (squatting) and despite the threat of Indian reprisals.

Although its demographic and economic potential was great and its territorial boundaries vast, the United States in the 1780s was far from a world power. No one knew that better, or more bitterly resented it, than the nation's diplomatic corps. Peace had not brought respect to the new nation. Benjamin Franklin, one of the architects of the Treaty of Paris, summed up the situation best. Franklin told Henry Laurens, another of the American negotiators in Paris, "I have never yet known of a peace that did not occasion a great deal of popular discontent, clamor, and censure on both sides." Though the diplomats were lauded at home, abroad John Adams found himself regarded with open distaste at the Court of St. James, to which he was posted after the peace. Thomas Jefferson, while treated better as American minister in Paris, made little headway gaining commercial advantages for the United States from the French crown. John Jay's experience during the war at the Spanish Court, followed by his failed efforts to gain a commercial treaty with Britain, left even this most patient and diplomatic diplomat at his wits' end. How could the new nation expect better from the great powers, given its internal disorder and its financial disarray, Jay wrote to a confidant on July 19, 1783. "The reluctance with which the states in general pay the necessary taxes [to the Congress] is much to be regretted. It injures both their reputation and interest abroad as well as at home, and tends to cherish the hopes and speculation of those who wish we may always be…an unimportant divided people."[31]

## Articles of Confederation

The job of getting the new states to work together troubled Congress, for the colonies had little precedent for an effective union of any kind. Even when the colonies were imperiled by France and its Indian allies, only five sent delegates to the Albany conference of 1754 to coordinate their defense. Any effective confederation plan faced two problems: first, how to divide power between the central government and the states, and second, how was the confederation government itself to operate? Again the task fell to the lawyers who had begun the Revolution, and first among them, John Dickinson.

Dickinson was selected to chair a committee to draft Articles of Confederation on July 2, 1776. The plan went to Congress on July 22, 1776, but Congress did not approve it until November 15, 1777, and then only after extensive debate and revision. Three-and-a-half years passed before Maryland, the final holdout, ratified the Articles, another evidence of interstate disunity. The Articles had a preface rather than a preamble: "Articles of Confederation and perpetual Union between the States of New Hampshire, Massachusetts-bay, Rhode Island and Providence Plantations, Connecticut, New York, New Jersey, Pennsylvania, Delaware, Maryland, Virginia, North Carolina, South Carolina and Georgia" (much like the formulation that Randolph would propose to the Constitutional Convention in June 1787). The confederation was to be perpetual. The next clause reasserted states' sovereignty. "Each State retains its sovereignty, freedom, and independence, and every power, jurisdiction, and right, which is not by this confederation expressly delegated to the United States in Congress assembled." Subsequent clauses indicated that the conduct of war and diplomacy were the exclusive province of Congress (as they had been in the Continental Congress). The Articles continued, "The said States hereby severally enter into a firm league of friendship with each other, for their common defense, the security of their liberties, and their mutual and general welfare, binding themselves to assist each other, against all force offered to, or attacks made upon them, or any of them, on account of religion, sovereignty, trade, or any other pretense whatever." How a league of friendship was also a perpetual union was a mystery until one realized that some of the framers of the Articles wanted a stronger central government while others would have preferred even less central authority. This disparity in opinion was allayed by the provision that important decisions of the Congress required nine states' approval (each state cast one vote in Congress), and that all changes to the Articles had to have unanimous consent of all thirteen state legislatures.

James Wilson was one of the framers of the Articles who wanted a stronger national government and less state autonomy.

He believed that the people of the nation were the true sovereigns, not the states. As he argued in a pamphlet defending the Bank of North America, in 1785, "the act of independence was made before the articles of confederation. This act [i.e., the declaring of independence] declares, that 'these united colonies' (not enumerating them separately) are free and independent...the confederation was not intended to weaken or abridge the powers and rights, to which the United States were previously entitled....The United States have general right, general powers, and general obligations, not derived from any particular states." But until 1786 Wilson and his fellow nationalists were in the minority.[32]

Under the Articles of Confederation the Congress depended on states for requisitions (financial gifts). It did not have an executive or judicial branch, although one might regard the Congress as more of a collective executive (after all, it made war and peace) than a legislature (for it lacked the power to tax). Most of its business was done in committee, some standing, like the committee on military affairs, some ad hoc, like the committees of safety created during the revolutionary agitation. Debates in it seemed endless to its members, though they could not serve for more than three years out of six.[33]

From its inception to its demise, the confederation ran red ink. The war cost over 150 million dollars, money that Congress had to borrow from creditors or request from the states. The Continental currency had "depreciated" (fallen) to 2 percent of its face value. Officers and men in the army waited to be paid, as did foreign creditors, including the governments of France and the Netherlands. Attempts by members of Congress to change the articles in order to raise a revenue failed when states like Rhode Island, fearing loss of their sovereignty to the larger states, vetoed the measures.

Congress turned to the Pennsylvania speculator and businessman Robert Morris to take charge of its finances. Robert Morris never did separate his own interests and dealings from those of the Congress, but he convinced Congress to give him powers over the treasury equal to those Washington had over the conduct of the war. With help from his loyal and astute deputy Gouverneur Morris, Robert formulated proposals for a national bank that would emit new bank notes, and for the solicitation of loans from Europe. His program favored his friends among the creditor classes, but it also would have put the new nation on a far sounder economic footing.

He was never given the chance to deploy his system, and a decade later would fall into the disgrace of debtor's prison when his creditors gave up waiting for him to pay his debts. Gouverneur Morris, a wilier investor, did better.[34]

The Congress could boast some successes. To regulate the process of settlement, a problem that would occupy national government well into the nineteenth century, Congress lobbied the states to surrender their western land claims to Congress, creating a national domain open to all American settlers. Reluctantly in some cases, the states acceded to this requirement. Congress then passed the Ordinance of 1784, allowing new territories to enter the United States on equal terms with the original thirteen states, and the Land Ordinance of 1785, providing for survey and division of the territory into square townships of sixteen "sections" (each a square mile). The land was to be sold at auction, under the assumption that entire townships would be purchased by communities moving west, thus insuring orderly settlement. In fact, the land was bought by speculators and resold to individual farmers, resulting in uncertainty and leaving many homesteaders with a crushing debt.

In 1787 another land ordinance barred slavery from states carved out of the Northwest Territory, free emigrants not wishing to compete with slave labor. The Ordinance of 1787 also created a political system for the region. In what would become the model for all the new territories, Congress appointed a governor and three judges and let adult male property holders elect a territorial legislature. When the population reached sixty thousand, the territory could apply for statehood and draft a temporary constitution. The Southwest Ordinance of 1790 would allow slavery in the national domain south of the Ohio River. But the entire process of land settlement was anything but tranquil.[35]

Delegates to the Congress well knew its debility, and the baleful influence this had on the common defense, the general welfare, the diplomacy, and the financial soundness of the new nation. Some begged for a stronger central government. For example, Connecticut no sooner sent lawyer William Samuel Johnson to Congress than he pleaded with the members to reform the Articles. The plan, broached in 1781, was to raise a revenue for the Congress from imposts (import duties). Even this plan failed, as New York, then

Rhode Island, then Virginia refused to agree, each state's refusal denying Congress the unanimous vote needed for the reform.[36]

Virginia had agreed at first. Its recantation bespoke some of its leaders' fear of a consolidated government, even after the proofs of the incapacity of the Congress mounted. The consolidation of outstanding state land claims in the west into a national domain particularly concerned Virginians, whose claims stretched to the Pacific Ocean. Mason reported to Thomas Jefferson, "You have, no doubt, been informed of the factious, illegal, and dangerous schemes now in contemplation in Congress [for ceding Virginia's western land claims to a national domain]…this power, directly contrary to the Articles of Confederation, is assumed upon the doctrine now industriously propagated that the late revolution has transferred the sovereignty formerly possessed by Great Britain to the United States, that is to the American Congress. A doctrine which, if not immediately arrested in its progress, will be productive of every evil." The evils included the loss of state autonomy first and the speculative value of western lands second.[37]

Mason was troubled by the weakness of the confederation, however, and, in a series of informal meetings with his neighbor and close friend George Washington, expressed the need for a reform of the Articles. At the very least some sort of cooperation beyond what existed was necessary in the navigation of the Potomac—a source of contention between Virginia and Maryland. Mason offered and Washington added his support for a meeting of delegates from the two states to resolve differences.

State authorities continued to have little use for the movement for reform, however. Thus Virginia's call for a meeting at Annapolis of delegates from all the states in September 1786 brought a response from only nine of them, and only five managed to send delegates—Virginia, Delaware, New Jersey, Pennsylvania, and New York. Maryland, whose capital was the site of the conference, sent no delegates. But Hamilton was there from New York, and Madison and Randolph represented Virginia. Their conversations began a collaboration that would bear fruit in Philadelphia the following year. One may even surmise that they conspired to replace the Articles with a more national form of government truly able to put down domestic violence.[38]

The Annapolis "Commissioners to Remedy Defects of the Federal Government" met for four days, from September 11 to 14, and Hamilton and Madison drafted a report to the Congress: "Deeply impressed…with the magnitude and importance of the object confided to them on this occasion, your Commissioners cannot forbear to indulge an expression of their earnest and unanimous wish, that speedy measures may be taken, to effect a general meeting, of the States, in a future Convention, for the same, and such other purposes, as the situation of public affairs, may be found to require." Something must be done; that much was clear to the self-styled commissioners. They could not or would not offer specifics but could agree "That there are important defects in the system of the Federal Government is acknowledged by the Acts of all those States, which have concurred in the present Meeting…from the embarrassments which characterize the present State of our national affairs, foreign and domestic." The revolutionaries were accustomed to holding conferences and meeting in conclaves, where "as may reasonably be supposed to merit a deliberate and candid discussion, in some mode, which will unite the Sentiments and Councils of all the States." The commissioners suggested "that a Convention of Deputies from the different States, for the special and sole purpose of entering into this investigation, and digesting a plan for supplying such defects" was appropriate. Then, proposals might be "particularized." Hamilton and Madison and the other delegates went home, sadder, no wiser, but hopeful that the Congress would call for another, more fully representative, meeting.[39]

Madison came away from the Annapolis meeting profoundly unsatisfied. He despised the weakness of the nation and the unwillingness of the states to remedy the situation. In March 1787, thirty-six years old and a veteran of Virginia politics, Madison had seen firsthand the failure of the confederation. "Not a single state complies with the requisitions [for revenue], several pass over them in silence, and some positively reject them.…It is not possible that a government can last long under these circumstances." Indeed Madison was rethinking the entire question of the "centralization" of government. Never as strong a nationalist as Alexander Hamilton or James Wilson, his views of the shape of government evolved as he took part in the Annapolis conference of 1786 and prepared for Virginia's role in the constitutional convention of 1787. As he wrote to Washington in April, 1787, "Conceiving that an individual independence of the states is utterly irreconcilable with their aggregate sovereignty; and that a consolidation of the whole into one simple republic would be as inexpedient as it is unattainable, I have sought for some middle ground, which may at once support a due supremacy of the national authority, and not exclude the local [i.e., state] authorities wherever they can be subordinately useful."[40]

## Shays's Rebellion

When the handful of delegates returned home from the Annapolis meeting, they received disquieting news from New England. There, farmers who could not pay debts or their back taxes and faced foreclosure on their mortgages were beginning public protests eerily similar to those of 1774. Then, angry patriots had closed the royal courts and refused to obey royal officials. Might the same farmers resist the elected officials of their own state governments? "Debt relief" governments elected in seven states after 1783 tried to help the farmers by delaying the collection of taxes, but nothing prevented private creditors from foreclosing on mortgages. The financial crisis grew worse when bad weather in 1784 caused widespread crop failures. By 1786, with western Massachusetts farmers losing their homesteads and the state government, dominated by eastern creditors, refusing to provide further relief, a former Continental Army captain named Daniel Shays and his allies led a tax revolt. "Shays's rebellion," as it was called, was ultimately quashed by military action in 1787, but the specter of rural unrest and local uprisings sent shivers of fear through the country. Indeed, indebted farmers in New Jersey and Virginia seemed likely to follow in Massachusetts' farmers' footsteps but stopped short of organized resistance to state government.[41]

Mounting dissonance between western, poorer farmers and eastern, wealthier creditor factions in the states, exacerbated by mal-apportioned electoral districts (favoring the coast over the hinterlands), reflected mounting friction over debt relief legislation, the emission of paper money (which would favor the debtor), the repayment of mortgage loans (held by the eastern banks), and control of the state legislatures and governors' offices. In all, conditions were ripe for domestic contention, if not outright violence.[42]

Violence came in 1786. Still weighed down by debt, Shays and his comrades petitioned the state assembly for relief and got a delay in the confiscation of their farms, but Shays and ten others were indicted for disorderly conduct. As they were led to Springfield for trial, the eleven men were joined by hundreds of others in sympathy with their plight. The judges, recognizing the danger to themselves, postponed the hearings and decamped. Governor James Bowdoin called out the militia to suppress the spreading tax revolt, and discovered to his horror that many of the militiamen marched with Shays. Samuel Adams, whose tactics in the revolutionary crisis resembled Shays's, was now concerned that "foreign agitators" were at work in western Massachusetts. Adams' fellow revolutionary, Bowdoin, was furious at the Shaysites' insult to the "dignity" of the government (a sentiment similar to one Thomas Hutchinson had expressed in 1773). A winter confrontation between Shays's forces and Bowdoin's hastily assembled state troops resulted in the flight of the rebels. Shays fled to Vermont, then an independent republic. Other leaders of the short-lived protest movement were tried, convicted, and, in all but two cases, pardoned by Bowdoin. By April, "the sense that government repression was too severe was growing. Even those who recognized the necessity of forcibly suppressing the rebellion regarded the mopping-up phase as misguided." Shays returned to Massachusetts in 1788 and was pardoned. He died on his farm in 1835. No monument marks his role in the coming of the Constitution.[43]

For his own part, Bowdoin was mortified by Shays's "highhanded offense" and denounced its "most fatal and pernicious consequences [that] must tend to subvert all law and government; dissolve our excellent Constitution, and introduce universal riot, anarchy, and confusion, which would probably terminate in absolute despotism, and consequently destroy the fairest prospects of political happiness." Watching the onset of the rebellion from Mount Vernon, to which he had retired after resigning his commission as commander-in-chief of the Continental army, Washington wrote to fellow planter and revolutionary war officer Henry ("Light-horse Harry") Lee, "The picture which you have exhibited, and the accounts which are published of the commotions, and temper of numerous bodies in the Eastern States, are equally to be lamented and deprecated. They exhibit a melancholy proof of what our trans-Atlantic foe has predicted; and of another thing perhaps, which is still more to be regretted, and is yet more unaccountable, that mankind when left to themselves are unfit for their own Government. I am mortified beyond expression when I view the clouds that have spread over the brightest morn that ever dawned upon any Country."[44]

................

Congress received the report of the Annapolis commissioners on September 20th, by which time the Shaysites' protests were well underway. Nothing was done in Congress—a common lament of its members—until February 20, 1787. Then a "grand committee" composed of one delegate from each state voted, by a bare majority, to ask Congress to ask the states to select delegates to a May convention in Philadelphia (a step Virginia's legislature had already taken independently). The next day, after more fustian, Congress issued a tepid invitation (scaling down the language and scaling back the proposal of the Hamilton/Madison report) to the states to gather in Philadelphia "for the sole and express purpose of revising the Articles of Confederation," advice that the delegates would report and recommend to Congress, and thence to the states whose autonomy Congress so carefully preserved. But many of the delegates to Congress already had other ideas. For even Congress had conceded that some changes were necessary "for the exigencies of government and the preservation of the Union." Just what those challenges were, and how they might be surmounted, was left to the delegates in May. Congress would say no more.[45]

......................

## CHAPTER 2

# The Constitutional Convention Meets

The confederation era had enshrined the ideal of government by "we the people" and illustrated at the same time the problems of disunion. In the years between the outbreak of the Revolutionary War and the call for a convention to revise the Articles of Confederation, the new nation confronted the weakness of the common defense and disputes over the meaning of general welfare. The blessings of liberty went unfulfilled for many, and state governments proved unable to insure domestic tranquility. The elusive goal of establishing justice remained just that—elusive. The call for a convention was almost a last resort, the same resort to which the patriots turned when they met in the Continental Congress. On that occasion, a meeting of the minds led to the Declaration of Independence and the Articles of Confederation. No one knew what the delegates to the Philadelphia conclave would achieve.

## "An Assembly of Demigods"

Somewhat facetiously, while both men were on diplomatic assignment in Europe, Thomas Jefferson described to John Adams the fifty-five delegates to the Convention as "an assembly of demi-gods." A secret deist, Jefferson did not believe in gods of any kind, and John Adams, a deeply religious Congregationalist, was skeptical that any gathering of men might think themselves godlike, but both were right that to the Philadelphia state house had come a selection of the best and the brightest political minds of their generation (absent Jefferson and Adams).[1]

James Madison, engraving from Gilbert Stuart painting, 1805.
*Courtesy of the Library of Congress, LC-DIG-hec-03838.*

James Madison was the engine that kept the convention in motion. Without his labors the convention might never have produced the Constitution. Madison had prodded the Virginia legislature to urge the Annapolis resolutions on the Congress. When the Congress asked the states to send delegates to a grand convention, in the late winter of 1787, James Madison's name was added to the Virginia delegation to the Philadelphia Convention. He took a stagecoach from New York City, where the Congress met, to Philadelphia. On May 5, alighting weary and bone sore (the roads were unpaved and the carriage had no shock absorbers), he found that he was the first non-Pennsylvanian to arrive. In a way, that was fitting, for he was already ahead of the delegates in his thinking. He roomed at Mary House's bed and breakfast along with a number of the other delegates, including Randolph. Madison's memories of an earlier stay there when the Congress sat in Philadelphia were bittersweet. He had courted the daughter of another delegate then, but never quite proposed, and later he found she was married to another man. But the time for recollections came to an abrupt end as the other delegates began to arrive.[2]

Madison's preparation for the meeting, based on his reading, his experience, and his logical mind, was superb. He came to Philadelphia ready to persuade the other delegates rather than just listen. Madison was not a lawyer, but he was well read in political philosophy, law, history, and related topics. Short, slight of build, conservatively dressed, Madison might have seemed lost as he moved about the state house hall. He was no orator, unlike King and Gouverneur Morris. He spoke quietly. But his authority derived from his mastery of any subject on which he spoke. Even before the convention formally met, "Madison fashioned a powerful and comprehensive analysis of the problems of federalism and republicanism." He "challenged accepted wisdom," compiled an exhaustive list of the shortcomings of the confederation, and most important, tackled the notion that a republic must be small to avoid the factions, corruption, and ultimate dissolution of great empires. Throughout the meetings of the various committees to which his fellow delegates routinely appointed him, Madison was the driving force behind the political cut and thrust, pressing for a sound and speedy resolution of disputes. His notes of the convention remain our foremost source on its deliberations. Rightly, history regards him as the "father" of the Constitution.[3]

Madison was joined on May 13th by George Washington, whose Mount Vernon home was just across the Potomac from Maryland. Without the presence of Washington, the convention could hardly have been effective; with him it could claim to be the last and most fitting act of the Revolution. Washington was to chair the convention, and his presence had a dampening effect on disputes. At first, he had mixed opinions about even attending. A steady stream of letters from John Jay and others, and a procession of visitors helped him make up his mind. But already in his fifties and worn from his long military service, Washington fell ill on his trip. Still, crowds came out to cheer him, and his customary reserve, added to the discomfort of his arthritis, must have been relieved by the esteem his countrymen showed him. At the edge of the city, he was met by his former officers and escorted to the state house, where Robert Morris offered his hospitality to the general. Washington accepted and stayed with the financier of the Revolution for the duration of the convention. He hated the humidity and the heat but enjoyed the hospitality of the city and presided over the sessions with Augustinian gravity. As the rules committee of the body (George Wythe, Alexander Hamilton, and Charles Cotesworth Pinckney) had proposed to keep its deliberations secret, he confided little of what transpired to his letters. Even his diary entries were confined to day-to-day irritations, of which, apparently, there were many.[4]

The other delegates drifted in during the final weeks of May and into June, an almost studied languor that service in Congress had taught them. Madison reported to Jefferson, "Monday last was the day for the meeting of the Convention. The number as yet assembled is but small. Among the few is Genl Washington who arrived on Sunday evening amidst the acclamations of the people, as well as more sober marks of the affection and veneration which continues

The State House in Philadelphia, 1776, by John Serz.
*Courtesy of the Library of Congress, LC-USZ62-17704*

to be felt for his character....There is a prospect of a pretty full meeting on the whole, though there is less punctuality in the outset than was to be wished." Madison did not mention that he used the time to advantage, caucusing with the other Virginia delegates as they arrived, roughing out what would be called the Virginia Plan.[5]

Alexander Hamilton arrived in the city amid little fanfare. He took his seat when the convention opened on May 25th, served on the rules committee and attended diligently until June 19th, and then returned at the end of August. Much respected for his keen intellect and his ability to frame large issues in clear and precise terms, he was also the most elusive of the delegates. His nationalism was plain—he had been the most outspoken advocate of a strong central government for nearly a decade. Thus his silence through the three weeks of the convention was uncharacteristic of this most outspoken and passionate of advocates. Even his demeanor seemed subdued.[6]

Gouverneur Morris was already in Philadelphia when Hamilton arrived. He watched with his characteristic amusement as the delegates sought lodgings. Though by now a man of considerable means himself, he did not act the host—that role went to Gouverneur's friend and patron, Robert Morris, and to Benjamin Franklin. But in the sessions of the convention Gouverneur was a force to be reckoned with, for when he spoke, and he did so often, he commanded the attention of the assembly. Physical presence, sheer size, mattered for the "tall boy."[7]

The delegates to the Constitutional Convention did not know if their labor would be successful. Some states' delegations maintained a discipline and voted as a bloc, while others, notably New York's, fractured and all but dissolved. The work of the convention included ingenious plans, elegant speeches, digressions, and diversions, and it moved in spurts and starts, moments of progress stymied by periodic stalemates, through all of which the business of constitution writing progressed fitfully.

## The Prospect of Union

In the middle of May 1787, when the delegates to the convention were trickling into Philadelphia, Madison was thinking hard on the subject of union. After all, it was the prime purpose of the gathering.

Madison would later admit to what he had planned for the convention all along. "The novelty of the undertaking immediately strikes us. It has been shewn in the course of these papers, that the existing Confederation is founded on principles which are fallacious; that we must consequently change this first foundation, and with it, the superstructure resting upon it."[8]

Madison may have been the first to plot the audacious step of going beyond mere amendment of the Articles to fabricate a more perfect union. He had seen, firsthand, the failure of the confederation. "Not a single state complies with the requisitions [for revenue], several pass over them in silence, and some positively reject them....It is not possible that a government can last long under these circumstances." Madison was quietly, as was his wont, rethinking the question of "centralization" of government. His views of the shape of government evolved as he took part in the Annapolis conference of 1786 and prepared for Virginia's role in the Constitutional Convention of 1787.[9]

The convention's consideration of union began, as so much did in the new nation, with people from Virginia, and the so-called Virginia plan that Governor Edmund Randolph presented on May 30th. He told the assemblage that "The articles of the Confederation should be so enlarged and corrected as to answer the purposes of the institution." The idea of union then was a corrective, vague in its generality, and hardly worth the title. Morris seconded the motion, and then the two men moved to substitute for their own motion a second motion, "resolved that a union of the states, merely federal, will not accomplish the objects posed by the article[s] of confederation, namely, 'common defense, security of liberty, and general welfare.'" One notes that Morris was already airing two of the key phrases of the final Preamble—common defense and general welfare. It was a bold step, so early in the convention, to press for a very different kind of union than a confederation. But no sooner had the resolution been read and seconded, than voices were raised against any "national" or "supreme" frame of government. Randolph and Morris, correctly sensing that they had been a little too bold too soon, agreed to postpone consideration of their second motion.[10]

The doubters soon revealed themselves: Elbridge Gerry of Massachusetts and George Mason did not like the look of the resolution at all, and Morris was soon on the defensive. But he would prove as indefatigable in defense as he was irrepressible on the offensive. "Morris explained the distinction between a federal and national, supreme government: the former being a mere compact resting on the good faith of the parties; the latter having a complete and compulsive operation." In short, the former was the confederation, with all its faults, the latter was where the convention must go—and he would take it there. One could say that he kept that promise sometime between September 8th and September 12th, when the Committee of Style reported its draft, but much had to happen before Morris would triumph.[11]

On June 13th, the committee of the whole agreed "that a national government ought to be established, consisting of a supreme legislative, judiciary, and executive." Two days later, William Paterson of New Jersey presented an alternative plan of government, shortly thereafter termed the New Jersey Plan, that would have given more limited powers to the new national government and protected the interests of the states with smaller populations. The plan featured a unicameral legislature with each state having equal representation, a federal executive officer elected for a one year term, and a high court with limited powers. No provision was made for inferior federal courts.[12]

Madison now faced a crisis of how to keep the convention moving in the face of the delegates' division over the very essence of union—small states' interests posed against large states' influence. Madison's solution was the committee system. Though long familiar to revolutionaries (in committees of correspondence and committees of safety the rebels undermined royal government, and the Continental Congress ran itself by committee; indeed it had many characteristics of a committee), the move to smaller committees reduced the likelihood that delegates would orate and increased the likelihood that they would bargain and negotiate. A committee of eleven delegates (one representative from each state present—the New Hampshire delegation did not arrive until late in July, and Rhode Island never sent a delegation) met on July 2nd to consider the problem of whether to base representation in the national legislature on population or on equal representation for each state. It reported on July 5th, and with some modifications its recommendations were adopted on July 16th in the "Great Compromise" that is the present House of Representatives and Senate.

On July 24th, the convention named a five-man Committee of Detail, including Edmund Randolph and James Wilson. It reported on August 4th, and its report was debated until the end of August. In the meantime, another committee of twelve was named to consider a proposal to assume all the state debts. (Although not adopted at that time, it became law in 1790.) On August 31st, all remaining matters of contention were assigned to the Committee on Postponed Matters (dubbed the Odds and Ends Committee), which David Brearley, Chief Justice of New Jersey, chaired. Another committee of eleven, it reported to the convention on September 3rd, and the delegates debated the report through the 5th. A last committee, termed the Committee of Style and Arrangement, was named on the 8th and reported on the 12th, and the debate and approval of its report concluded the work of the convention.

## Hamilton Speaks of Liberty and Faction

Madison feared that the liberties that Union would protect were prey to an insidious enemy within the body of delegates. If division became faction, liberty would be the victim. No keyword was ever more facilely associated with the American Revolution than "liberty." The concept, so plain to the founders, had a more complex history than their energetic praise of liberty revealed. For under colonial charters and in the English lexicon, liberty had a constellation of meanings rather than a unitary one, and those meanings limited rather than released the individual to do as he pleased. Liberty was freedom from illegal imprisonment. Liberty was a grant or "privilege" that law conferred, not a right in nature that belonged to men. Thus, for example, the franchise was a liberty restricted to men of property; liberties were protected by legislative bodies, not declarations or bills of rights; and democracy endangered liberty because liberty could not survive disorder that democracy supposedly brought in its wake. "Rights and liberties" were part of a hierarchical array of duties, obligations, and obedience to authority. Liberty did not free anyone; it simply defined where they fit in the social and political order.[13]

The Revolution altered this constellation of meanings. Liberty became a positive right rather than just a restraint on arbitrary government. It was this liberty that Jefferson extolled in the Declaration of Independence, that Benjamin Franklin referred to as the "blessings of liberty" in the Pennsylvania Bill of Rights, and that John Adams added to the Massachusetts Constitution of 1780—a liberty that was so fundamental that its roots were in nature and nature's law. As Adams wrote in his 1787 *A Defense of the Constitutions of Government of the United States*, liberty was a state of mind, a "tranquility...arising from the opinion each person has of his own safety." There could be no sense of safety, no liberty, if any branch of government were able to impose its force on the citizen arbitrarily. So Madison depicted the separation of powers in revolutionary constitutions: "No political truth is certainly of greater intrinsic value, or is stamped with the authority of more enlightened patrons of liberty, than that on which the objection is founded." When the Marquis de Lafayette died in 1834, Edward Everett of Massachusetts was one of the eulogists. He told the solemn gathering at Faneuil Hall, in Boston, "Thus the great principle of your revolutionary fathers, of your pilgrim sires, the great principle of the age, was the rule of his life: the love of liberty protected by law."[14]

The enemy of liberty that came first to the revolutionary generation's mind was "faction" and its consequent disunity. Faction was the enemy of liberty because it perverted liberty, allowing men in government to mistake self-interest for liberty. The founders agreed that the blessings that liberty bestowed on free men were always prone to corruption that faction fostered. Corruption fueled discontent and undermined unity.

The concept of faction the founders accepted was English in origin. Even as faction flourished in the partisan parliamentary politics of the eighteenth century, every English political writer denounced it. At best a faction was a self-interest party; at worst it was a treasonous cabal. Of course, politicians always accused their opponents of factionalism. To those in power, faction was identified with the opponents of government. To those seeking office, those in power were a faction. Almost infinitely malleable in its power to castigate one's rivals, faction was always bad. To the American revolutionaries, faction was the insidious enemy of liberty. Thus the loyalists were regarded as a faction; the patriots styled themselves "the people." That conclusion persisted into the late 1790s, even as temporary and shifting factions were morphing into what moderns would recognize as stable national political parties, the very men who led them continued to speak of the evils of faction.[15]

In different but overlapping ways, Washington, Madison, and Hamilton had already experienced the perils of faction. Faction had more than once threatened Washington's success as commander-in-chief during the war, as short-sighted members of Congress conspired with ambitious general officers to replace Washington. To his dying day, Washington resented faction. As his Farewell Address of 1796 warned, "All obstructions to the execution of the laws, all combinations and associations, under whatever plausible character, with the real design to direct, control, counteract, or awe the regular deliberation and action of the constituted authorities, are destructive of this fundamental principle, and of fatal tendency. They serve to organize faction, to give it an artificial and extraordinary force; to put, in the place of the delegated will of the nation the will of a party…to make the public administration the mirror of the ill-concerted and incongruous projects of faction, rather than the organ of consistent and wholesome plans digested by common counsels and modified by mutual interests."[16]

Madison espied faction everywhere. "By a faction I understand a number of citizens, whether amounting to a majority or minority of the whole, who are united and actuated by some common impulse of passion, or of interest, adverse to the rights of other citizens, or to the permanent and aggregate interests of the community." Faction tore apart the fabric of republican self-government. As he wrote in December, 1787, in the midst of the ratification debates, "Among the numerous advantages promised by a well constructed Union, none deserves to be more accurately developed than its tendency to break and control the violence of faction. The friend of popular governments, never finds himself so much alarmed for their character and fate, as when he contemplates their propensity to this dangerous vice."[17]

Serving at Washington's side through the war, Hamilton had seen faction when Washington's subordinates plotted against him and cliques in Congress conspired against the commander in chief. He had seen how "a zeal for liberty more ardent than enlightened" suborning such factions nearly cost the United States its existence. For Hamilton, factionalism cost all men real liberty.[18]

On June 18th Hamilton at last rose to speak. Standing erect, his clothing neat and fashionable, he commanded everyone's attention. He spoke for five hours without a break, truly a marathon performance. Years later, some of those who were in the chamber

Alexander Hamilton, by John Trumbull, 1792.
*Courtesy of the Library of Congress, LC-DIG-det-4a31480.*

and many of those who heard tell of Hamilton's oration, called him
a monarchist. He surely had little patience for the Virginia or the
New Jersey Plan. He wanted a strong central government with a
powerful executive branch. But Hamilton's real concern was the
same as Washington's and Madison's—faction, and the ill effect that
faction had upon liberty.[19]

Hamilton had taken the revolutionary generation's concern with
political licentiousness to heart. He told his fellow delegates that he
"had been hitherto silent on the business before the Convention,
partly from respect to others whose superior abilities age & experience rendered him unwilling to bring forward ideas dissimilar to
theirs, and partly from his delicate situation with respect to his own
State, to whose sentiments as expressed by his Colleagues, he could
by no means accede." The other New York delegates, Robert Yates
and John Lansing of Albany, opposed any central government and

would oppose ratification. They outvoted Hamilton. He must have been seething for days by the time he rose to speak. "The crisis however which now marked our affairs, was too serious to permit any scruples whatever to prevail over the duty imposed on every man to contribute his efforts for the public safety & happiness. He was obliged therefore to declare himself unfriendly to both plans."[20]

Madison's notes reported that Hamilton "was particularly opposed to that [plan] from N[ew] Jersey, being fully convinced, that no amendment of the Confederation, leaving the States in possession of their Sovereignty, could possibly answer the purpose. On the other hand, he confessed he was much discouraged by the amazing extent of Country in expecting the desired blessings from any general sovereignty that could be substituted." Liberty could not be sustained without government. Surely everyone understood that after the years of confederation government had suborned all manner of corruption and disorder. What had blinded his fellow delegates to so obvious a need? The answer was their own excessive love of liberty. "As to the powers of the Convention, he thought the doubts started on that subject had arisen from distinctions & reasonings too subtle." They entertained themselves with subtleties and frivolous displays of learning and logic. Behind these, however, were the very corruptions that undid liberty in every republic in history. Local interest, self interest, state interests—too much liberty prevented them from seeing the danger to liberty.

But Hamilton had not worked on his address for weeks without allowing himself a little discursive latitude on matters of history. He had from childhood been an avid reader, and history was high on his list of required readings. "A federal Govt. he conceived to mean an association of independent Communities into one. Different Confederacies have different powers, and exercise them in different ways." A truly federal system was one in which the independent communities surrendered some of their liberty, just as individuals must surrender some of their liberty to live in a political society. Better than the New Jersey Plan, "The plan last proposed [the Virginia Plan] departs itself from the federal idea, as understood by some, since it is to operate eventually on individuals." For sovereignty meant no more or less—the rightful authority of governments to act directly on their citizens. But this was not a federal idea, so far as he understood it. If such a government was to have any effect, it must not operate through the agency of another government. It must be sovereign over its territory.

He offered one concession to the Virginia Plan. "He agreed moreover with the Hon[ora]ble gentleman from Va. [Randolph] that we owed it to our Country, to do on this emergency whatever we should deem essential to its happiness. The States sent us here to provide for the exigencies of the Union." Hamilton's own state had not exactly done that—it had merely obeyed the far weaker invitation from the Congress to remedy the Articles. But Hamilton had written the far stronger Annapolis Conference report, and he must have been referring to it. "To rely on & propose any plan not adequate to these exigencies, merely because it was not clearly within our powers, would be to sacrifice the means to the end." Forget about the instructions the Congress had issued, he averred; they were faulty. "It may be said that the States can not ratify a plan not within the purview of the article of Confederation providing for alterations & amendments." But no matter, for here the delegates might take the liberty of proposing an entirely new structure of government, "in view a reference to the people at large."

For Hamilton, who was born in poverty in a place filled with slaves, liberty had a deeper personal meaning than it may have had to those born to wealth and status. Liberty was something that was won by valor, by daring, and by force of will. Liberty was earned, not assumed. Easily corrupted by vanity or by the promise of lucre, liberty had to be refreshed by a sense of honor, something that Hamilton had absorbed from the very highest traditions of military service. Above all, there could be no liberty without order. Ungoverned liberty was a vice, breeding other licentious vices.

Unlike Morris, whose outspokenness by day was matched by a delightful wit and genuine camaraderie when the day's work was done, or Madison, who would never give offense if he could avoid it, or King, whose probity and seriousness barred him from saying what he really thought, or Johnson, who personally preferred accommodation to controversy, Hamilton took no prisoners. Liberty was never without a price. The delegates must understand that.

If the two plans on the floor for debate were fatally flawed, as he thought, Hamilton returned the discussion to the basics. "The great question is what provision shall we make for the happiness of our Country?" Washington, sitting in the chair, might have ruled that Hamilton was no longer speaking to the motion, that is, making relevant comments, but Washington was Hamilton's patron, and no gentleman in the chamber called Hamilton out on his sweeping digression through history, political theory, and philosophy. A lecture on the nature of government followed—hours of it, longer than a college week's classroom sessions laid end to end.

Hamilton was a realist, sometimes painfully so. His own life had been full of pain—an absentee father, a mother dying young, penury relieved by the kindness of strangers, the move from the safety of college in New York City to the cold winters of Valley Forge. He pulled no punches when he laid out "The great & essential principles necessary for the support of Government" as "1. an active & constant interest in supporting it. This principle does not exist in the States in favor of the federal Govt.... They constantly pursue internal interests adverse to those of the whole" and "2. The love of power. Men love power.... The ambition of [the states'] demagogues is known to hate the controul of the Genl. Government."

The love of power corroded true liberty, for power at bottom was nothing but "a coertion of laws or coertion of arms." Government could not exist without this power, but uncontrolled, it was the enemy of good government. "A certain portion of military force is absolutely necessary in large communities.... But how can this force be exerted on the States collectively. It is impossible. It amounts to a war between the parties." Without a national government, the states would war with one another, their liberties conflicting with those of their neighbors.

How might liberty be saved in such a situation? Starry-eyed references to civic virtue and disinterested patriotism did not appeal to Hamilton. Instead he discoursed on "Influence; [I do] not mean corruption, but a dispensation of those regular honors & emoluments, which produce an attachment to the Govt." Honors kept liberty in balance with power. But the states could not provide such an ordered liberty, for "all the passions then we see, of avarice, ambition, interest, which govern most individuals, and all public bodies, fall into the current of the States." For this reason, any federation based on the New Jersey Plan "will & must fail...and the Union itself be dissolved."

Hamilton foresaw how the large states would respond to the New Jersey Plan, a response based on political calculation (popular representation in the federal government would give more power to the more populous states), but his own argument rested not so much on his experience in politics as his reading of human nature. "It is not in human nature that Va. & the large States should consent to it [the New Jersey Plan], or if they did that they shd. long abide by it. It shocks too much the ideas of Justice, and every human feeling." Just as a healthy human nature required a balance of liberty with order, so a healthy polity required a balance of liberty and order.

Only in a general government would Americans find this balance. "He was persuaded that great oeconomy might be obtained by substituting a general Govt. He did not mean however to shock the public opinion by proposing such a measure. On the other hand he saw no other necessity for declining it." The states were not "necessary for any of the great purposes of commerce, revenue, or agriculture." A division of the whole into "Subordinate authorities he was aware would be necessary but...the vast & expensive apparatus now appertaining to the States" was a luxury that a nation faced with internal disorder and external enemies could not afford.

Hamilton went further. He proposed a familiar infamous model for a great nation over a vast expanse of territory, even though conventional wisdom taught that a republic could not govern an extensive territory. "In his private opinion he had no scruple in declaring, supported as he was by the opinions of so many of the wise & good, that the British Govt. was the best in the world: and that he doubted much whether any thing short of it would do in America. He hoped Gentlemen of different opinions would bear with him in this, and begged them to recollect the change of opinion on this subject which had taken place and was still going on." Not likely. The silence in the room must have been deafening. But how could vice be controlled when liberty was everywhere uncontrolled? The "progress of the public mind led him to anticipate the time, when others as well as himself would join in the praise...[of] the British Constitution, namely, that it is the only Govt. in the world 'which unites public strength with individual security.'" More silence—perhaps now broken by murmurs of disagreement. Hamilton soldiered on. "Give all power to the many, they will oppress the few. Give all power to the few, they will oppress the many." Liberty must be balanced, licentiousness contained. "To the proper adjustment of it the British owe the excellence of their Constitution." Once praised by

Enlightenment political theorists like Montesquieu and Voltaire, and extolled by loyalists who gloried in the successes of British arms and the excellence of British laws, the very mention of Britain was now distasteful to the company surrounding Hamilton. Madison must have been squirming, his own opinions of national government not far from Hamilton's, but their common aim endangered by Hamilton's reference to the former imperial master.

Hamilton looked about, hoping that he had some allies, knowing that was unlikely, and pressed forward. "He appealed to the gentlemen from the N. England States whether experience had not there verified the remark[s]." Had not Massachusetts in Shays's Rebellion demonstrated how important a strong executive was to the security of property and life? Well, perhaps, but Hamilton now went about as far as he could safely go into the English example, or perhaps too far. For his next step would dog him throughout his career. "Was not this giving up the merits of the question: for can there be a good Govt. without a good Executive. The English model was the only good one on this subject. The Hereditary interest of the King was so interwoven with that of the Nation, and his personal emoluments so great, that he was placed above the danger of being corrupted from abroad—and at the same time was both sufficiently independent and sufficiently controuled, to answer the purpose of the institution at home."

Every one of the revolutionaries believed that George III had been corrupted by his own ministers and his own ill-temper. He had declared the patriot lawyers traitors and sent troops to crush American liberties. Hamilton knew this, but it did not faze him. "It will be objected probably, that such an Executive will be an elective Monarch, and will give birth to the tumults which characterize that form of Govt. He would reply that Monarch is an indefinite term. It marks not either the degree or duration of power."

With all his criticism of the other plans concluded, Hamilton read "a sketch of a plan which he should prefer to either of those under consideration." The plan included a presidency for good behavior and a consolidated national government in which the states would be administrative districts. "He was aware that it went beyond the ideas of most members." That was an understatement. But the alternative he foresaw was a "Union dissolving or already dissolved." If he had gone too far beyond public opinion, "the people will in time be unshackled from their prejudices; and whenever that happens, they will themselves not be satisfied at stopping where the plan of Mr. R[andolph] would place them, but be ready to go as far at least as he proposes."

Hamilton finished with the fading light, and if he registered the response of the delegates (for he did not always allow himself to take others' feelings into account), he might have seen the dismay on their faces. A faint scattering of applause closed the session. Though his proposals for a lifetime executive and his desire to abolish state governments surely led the list of odious proposals, these were not real concerns of the rest of the delegates. No one was going to subscribe to a constitution that created an elective kingship or did away with the states' sovereignty. Why then had he bothered? When Hamilton thought he was right, the opinions of others mattered little to him. Hamilton's oration was fearless. He did not court popularity. He said what he thought.

## Compromises

Hamilton was never much of a compromiser, and as the debate over the two plans grew as hot as the late June afternoons, he went back to New York to manage his law practice. But others were trying to cool the temperature inside the assembly hall by offering what would in time be called the Great Compromise. Roger Sherman of Connecticut had offered it on June 20th, and his colleague William Samuel Johnson repeated it on June 29th: Let the lower house be apportioned according to population along the lines of the Virginia Plan and the upper house of the new government follow the New Jersey plan of equal representation for each state. On July 16th, advocates of the compromise had gained enough votes, though its proponents had only a bare majority (five states for it, four opposed, one abstaining). At first, Madison hotly opposed the compromise, but he later reconciled himself to it. As he explained in defense of the new constitution some months later, the Great Compromise insured that the new government would be a federal one, with the federal government's powers enumerated and the states' powers reserved to them. The key lay in the proposal that "The Senate...will derive its powers from the States, as political and coequal societies; and these will be represented on the principle of equality in the Senate, as they now are in the existing Congress." Characteristically, in convincing himself to compromise, Madison brilliantly turned his doubts about the capacities of state governments into a defense of the principle of dual or shared sovereignty between the states and the federal government.[21]

A second compromise at the convention occasioned even more recrimination than the Great Compromise. Slavery was legal throughout the South in 1787. A few of the northern states had ended it, and a few more were debating or had passed gradual emancipation laws. But everyone was clear on the central fact that slavery was determined by state law. There was no reason, thus, for it to be discussed in a federal constitution, and it might have gone simply without mention as the delegates were fashioning the document. But as Madison presciently told the delegates during the debate over the Great Compromise, the real divide in the new nation lay not between large and small states, but between those states having slaves and those that had abandoned slavery.[22]

At the convention, Madison, Washington, and Hamilton avoided the issue of slavery. Washington owned many slaves, though his will freed his slaves and after his death his wife Martha manumitted them. He had no children to whom they might pass and no debts they might be sold to pay. Madison too owned slaves, and he feared slavery as an institution. "I take no notice," he wrote, of the "unhappy species of population" who might, given the opportunity, join in tempestuous scenes of civil violence." Such delicacy was typical of him in a state "abounding" in slaves, and he was well aware of the British threat to arm runaway slaves and pit them against their former masters during the war. For might not the slaves "emerge into the human character, and give a superiority of strength to any party with which they may associate themselves"? Hamilton had seen slavery in the West Indies in its cruelest form. He believed nothing so corrupted the liberty that free men enjoyed so much as the absolute dominion they exercised over their slaves. He would become a founding member of the New York Anti-Slavery Society. But for now, he was silent.[23]

Should they have spoken? They knew that in law, slavery was the antithesis of liberty. Slavery meant obedience to the will of another. Liberty meant the ability to exercise one's own will. Thus political liberty meant the power to exert one's will on the course of politics through speaking, writing, voting, and running for office. In slavery, the master's power was arbitrary. Liberty was a tranquility of mind, a condition no slave in his or her right mind might entertain. In a regime of liberty, the power of the state was regulated and limited by laws to which the citizen had consented. Thus the British impositions on the protesting colonists, for example the Boston Port Act (closing the port) in 1774, were accounted slavery by the merchants who used the port to engage in the Atlantic slave trade. So, too, at the Constitutional Convention, Southern delegates might inveigh against the slavery imposed by other states, for example in assigning the taxing power to Congress—without, to be sure, mentioning the word *slavery*. The language of liberty was filled with such contradictions in the era of the founders.[24]

Slavery raised the very specter of disorder that had brought many of the delegates to the Pennsylvania State House in the first place, though the fear of slave rebellion was, in all probability, far greater than the reality. After all, in all of the slave colonies of the mainland, there had only been three major rebellions from 1608 to 1776, two in New York City, in 1712 and 1741, and one in South Carolina, in 1739. But the fear of slave rebellion was another matter entirely. No master could afford to ignore it—or did.[25]

Even as the delegates assembled, bands of runaway slaves in the deep South were coming together in frontier communities much like the "maroon" communities of slaves on the British sugar islands in the Caribbean. One simply could not ignore slavery if one walked the streets of Philadelphia that spring and summer. The state had passed a gradual emancipation law, but slavery was still legal. Twenty-five of the delegates owned slaves. Washington and Mason of Virginia both brought slaves with them to Philadelphia, as in all likelihood did members of the other southern delegations. Of course, there was the danger that, so close to freedom, slaves would vote with their feet for freedom (for Philadelphia was one stopping place for them on the way north), convincing some delegates like Madison to leave their bondsmen home.[26]

The debate over slavery at the convention began innocently enough, on June 11th, as part of the debate over the basis of representation in the new Congress. James Wilson suggested the obvious—the population of the states would determine the number of seats in the House of Representatives. Edward Rutledge of South Carolina then added the idea that allocation should not be based solely on the exercise of right to vote, that is, on freedom. Wilson then amended his proposal to the formula of counting "white and other free citizens" and "three-fifths of all other persons not comprehended in the foregoing language." It was assumed that free women would count in the apportionment of seats, even though they could not vote for the holders of those seats. Slavery, not sexual inequality, was on their minds. Behind the scenes a deal had been struck—the slave states agreed with the populous states on a plan to empower slavery, though not by name, in the Constitution. In Article I, Section 2, paragraph 3, as it would finally read: "Representatives and direct taxes shall be apportioned among the several states which may be included within this Union, according to their respective numbers, which shall be determined by adding the whole number of free persons, including those bound to service for a term of years, and excluding Indians not taxed, three-fifths of all other persons." The Three-Fifths Compromise gave to the slave South far more power in the legislative and executive branches of the federal government than they would have had without counting slaves at all.[27]

Equally important, this was the first—and in many senses the only—way in which the Constitution made distinctions in persons. (Though officers were routinely referred to as "he" in the Constitution, later federal case law stipulated that the male pronoun was generic rather than specific to men.) In light of the Three-fifths Compromise, "We the People" was not one, but two—white and other free citizen persons, and slaves. Wilson knew that Pennsylvania had many free blacks and that the state's constitution regarded the free blacks as citizens, so his proposal was not racist on its face. Chief Justice Roger Taney would make that connection in 1857 with *Dred Scott v. Sanford* (though the association of dark skin and slavery was hardly new in 1857, or in 1787 for that matter).

Elbridge Gerry of Massachusetts saw the plan in its inception and objected. Slaves were property, were they not? Southern state law made them chattel—like horses or cattle. Why not then count three-fifths of the livestock in the free states? "No one answered...the deal had been made." A quick calculation (though the decennial Census mandated by the Constitution would not take place until 1790) gave the slave states an additional twelve seats in Congress—a nice haul. The Great Compromise, allotting two senators to each state, would reconcile the smaller states to the Three-Fifths Compromise[28]

On August 7th, when the Committee of Detail reported, the Three-Fifths Compromise was not mentioned explicitly enough for the Southern delegates. This brought slavery front and center at the convention. When Rufus King warned that including approval of slavery in the Constitution, even by implication, "was a most grating circumstance" that would prove divisive in the future, Gouverneur Morris would not let the matter rest. He added that slavery was "a nefarious institution—it was the curse of heaven on the states where it prevailed." Including three-fifths of the slave population in the calculation of seats was compounding an abomination. "The inhabitant of Georgia and South Carolina who goes to the Coast of Africa, and in defiance of the most sacred laws of humanity tears away his fellow creatures from their dearest connections and damns them to the most cruel bondages, shall have more votes in a government instituted for the protection of the rights of mankind, than the citizen of Pennsylvania or New Jersey who views with a laudable horror so nefarious a practice." Morris's father had slaves, but Gouverneur had freed them and then argued for what eventually became New York State's gradual emancipation law (though that lay in the future).[29]

What eventually became Article IV also contained another of the comprises over slavery, the so-called Rendition Clause. Slavery was not mentioned in it, but everyone at the convention and in the states who read it knew what it implied. "No Person held to Service or Labour in one State, under the Laws thereof, escaping into another, shall, in Consequence of any Law or Regulation therein, be discharged from such Service or Labour, but shall be delivered up on Claim of the Party to whom such Service or Labour may be due." This answered the problem of runaway slaves, ancillary to any rebellion (in all previous rebellions some of the suspected culprits simply left the scene, hoping to escape punishment, while the instigators were often suspected runaways).

The Rendition Clause was not a major issue in the ratification debates, nor was the Three-Fifths Clause. In fact, the many compromises made in favor of slavery were not a prime concern of the antifederalists. Perhaps because so many of them came from the South, and viewed abolition with alarm, they did not even mention slavery. One Philadelphia newspaper satirically included it in the "blessings of liberty" the Constitution insured, but the northern federalists, including John Jay and Alexander Hamilton, both of whom opposed slavery, said nothing of it in the newspaper pieces they wrote explaining the Constitution's clauses. During the war, Hamilton proposed freeing slaves who joined the Continental forces, "for the dictates of humanity, and true policy, equally interest me in favor of this unfortunate class of men," but Hamilton kept his anti-slavery views to himself even after Gerry, King, and Morris had expressed theirs. Jay was well aware of the inconsistency of his own views. As he wrote to the English Society for Promoting the Manumission of Slaves, in June 1788, "That they who know the value of liberty, and are blessed with the enjoyment of it, ought not to subject others to slavery, is, like most other moral precepts, more generally admitted in theory than observed in practice." At the same time, "Permit us, however, to observe, that although consequences ought not to deter us from doing what is right, yet that it is not easy to persuade men in general to act on that magnanimous and disinterested principle. It is well known that errors, either in opinion or practice, long entertained or indulged, are difficult to eradicate, and particularly so when they have become, as it were, incorporated in the civil institutions and domestic economy of a whole people."[30]

Madison later defended the Three-Fifths Compromise in a set of newspaper essays. Depending on how one looks at his explanation, as either delicately tactful or masterfully obscurantist, the contrived disinterestedness of it showed how uncomfortable he was with the issue. To distance himself from the criticism of the clause, he adopted a rhetorical device: a dialogue between two people taking opposite sides of the issue. In fact, Madison did not give equal weight to the two sides. The question he posed was: ought "slaves to be included in the numerical rule of representation?" The real question was whether the Constitution gave some additional weight to slave states determining representation in Congress (and consequently in the electoral college that selected the president). As well, the Three-Fifths Clause made slavery a fundamental tenet of the new federal system. Madison wanted to skirt this second question, so the opponent of the Three-Fifths Clause in his two-character playlet objected not to slavery's impact on the Constitution but to slaves being counted as people. The objection went like this: Slaves are considered as property, not as persons, in Southern state law. They ought therefore to be comprehended in estimates of taxation which are founded on property, and to be excluded from representation which is regulated by a census of persons. (Note that this objection was not to slavery in itself.)[31]

The other character is the dialogue was "one of our southern brethren." He "subscribe[d] to the doctrine…that representation relates more immediately to persons, and taxation more immediately to property, and we join in the application of this distinction to the case of our slaves." Every Southerner, white or black, knew that slaves were people. Hence they should be added to the population of slave states when representatives to Congress were apportioned. But Madison's southern "brother" considered slavery in a denatured and abstract form. There was no ethical sensibility in Madison's description, though it went on for pages. Slavery was not evil. Slavery was not a positive good. Slavery was what it was. "This is in fact their true character. It is the character bestowed on them by the laws under which they live." Bestowed not by nature or by God, as it happened, but by Madison's "southern" spokesman.

Madison was happy to leave the subject of slavery as it was and return to the subject of representation. No longer the social observer, he resumed his role as the political realist: "It is agreed on all sides, that numbers are the best scale of wealth and taxation, as they are the only proper scale of representation. Would the convention have been impartial or consistent, if they had rejected the slaves from the list of inhabitants, when the shares of representation were to be calculated, and inserted them on the lists when the tariff of contributions was to be adjusted? Could it be reasonably expected, that the Southern States would concur in a system, which considered their slaves in some degree as men, when burdens were to be imposed, but refused to consider them in the same light, when advantages were to be conferred?"

. . . . . . . . . . . . . . . .

The debate over slavery encapsulated moral as well as political differences among the delegates. More ominously, it foretold a sectional divide in America that might, in the fullness of time and geographical expansion, imperil the Union itself. For now it was only a cloud in the sky that a man could cover with one hand, but the slavery debate made all the more necessary some statement of the desire for security and well-being, for the blessings of freedom and the imperatives of justice, and above all for the sovereignty of the entire people of the new nation. Gouverneur Morris would soon have the chance to do just that when the Committee on Style met.

## CHAPTER 3

# Drafting the Preamble

On September 8, 1787, Madison recorded in his notes, "A Committee was then appointed by Ballot to revise the stile of and arrange the articles which had been agreed to by the House. The committee consisted of Mr. Johnson, Mr. Hamilton, Mr. Govr. Morris, Mr. Madison and Mr. King." On the same day an attempt to revise the number of members of the House of Representatives gained Madison's and Hamilton's support, but it was defeated. The draft went to the committee without further ado, its charge to perfect the language creating the new federal system. By their balloting, the convention members placed their faith in colleagues who had shown the drive and ability to perform this final task.[1]

In eighteenth-century thought, perfection in political systems was often sought but rarely achieved. Eighteenth-century political theory, "an uneasy amalgam of classical maxims of government, narrow partisan polemics, antiquarian learning, historical researches and technical legal doctrine," was hardly capable of envisioning perfection. Indeed, one theme in the body of precepts, narratives, and ideologies stood out: the inevitable decline and fall of every system of government. No system was perfect because none was proof against the failings of rulers and the weakness of peoples. The most frail of these political systems were republics, and convention held that the larger the republic, the sooner faction would undermine and topple it. As Hamilton warned, "is it not time to awake from the deceitful dream of a gold age and to adopt a practical maxim for the direction of our political conduct that we, as well as the other inhabitants of the globe are yet remote from the happy empire of perfect wisdom and perfect virtue?" Madison, too, worried that "the regular symmetry which an abstract view of the subject [of making constitutions] might lead an ingenious theorist to bestow on a Constitution" of such a document could only be "planned in his closet or in his imagination."[2]

The genius of the Committee of Style lay precisely in its bold reply to conventional pessimism about constitutions and republics. In its hands, the impossibility of a perfect union became the command to create "a more perfect union" and the fear that all republics were doomed they transformed into the hope that "our posterity" would honor and preserve the Constitution. It is thus especially unfortunate that historians have very little evidence of what went on in the meetings of the Committee of Style. Madison was present, but his pen, kept busy keeping notes all through the convention, did not record the committee's deliberations. Thus one must reconstruct the thinking of the committee members from what they said and wrote before and after the five days.

## From Preface to Preamble

The so-called New Jersey Plan had a preface: "That the articles of confederation ought to be so revised, corrected and enlarged as to render the federal constitution adequate to the exigencies of government and the preservation of the union." Randolph's initial formulation of a preamble was an answer to Paterson's but did not go beyond the functions of government to discuss its purposes. "The object of our preamble ought to be briefly to declare that the present federal government is insufficient to the general happiness; that the conviction of this fact gave birth to this Convention; and that the only effectual mode which they can devise for curing this insufficiency is the establishment of a supreme legislative, executive, and judiciary. Let it be next declared that the following are the Constitution and fundamentals of government for the United States." One can see in the wording Randolph's implication that the New Jersey Plan was not an adequate remedy to the defects of the Articles of Confederation. But if "A preamble seems proper for the purpose of designating the ends of government and human policies," it should still not be some scholarly display of "theory, howsoever proper in the first formation of state governments," because there were already state governments. Nor "yet is it proper for the purpose of mutually pledging the faith of the parties," a legal convention often seen in private contractual dealings that had found its way into state constitutional preambles.[3]

On August 6th, the Committee of Detail agreed upon a preamble: "We the people of the states of New-Hampshire etc. do ordain, declare, and establish the following frame of government of the United States." Later, all the states were named, including Rhode Island, though it had no representatives at the convention; New York, two of whose three representatives had gone home to lobby against the new draft; and North Carolina, which, with Rhode Island, failed to ratify the Constitution until after it went into effect. Also, the closing phrase "for the government of ourselves and our posterity" appeared. The last was in the handwriting of James Wilson, not Randolph, and hinted at Wilson's more robust nationalism. But the phrase, taken as a whole, was still "we the people of the states of." Madison copied the report of the committee of detail into his journal, and he had the same language for the preamble. It was nothing more than an introduction. It had no substance of its own. The next day, the preamble was agreed to unanimously by the committee of the whole, it appearing to say nothing offensive to any delegation.[4]

On September 8th, the newly created Committee of Style met to prepare the final version of the Constitution. The delegates would then vote on it and, if it passed, it would be sent to the Congress sitting in New York City, and hopefully by the Congress (for nothing forced the Congress to this step) to the various states for ratification. The process for the latter and final step was spelled out in Article VII of the draft itself—"The ratification of the conventions of nine states, shall be sufficient for the establishment of this Constitution between the states so ratifying the same." It mandated that the states call special conventions to ratify the Constitution. The delegates wanted to avoid, if at all possible, a constitution that curtailed state sovereignty going directly to the various state legislatures. What is more, ratification by convention (on the Massachusetts constitutional model of 1780) more closely conformed to the ideal of popular sovereignty embodied in "We the People." Finally, ratification did not require unanimous consent of the thirteen states—a problem reformers of the Articles had faced repeatedly.[5]

William Samuel Johnson, etching by Albert Rosenthal after painting by Gilbert Stuart.
*Courtesy of the Library of Congress, LC-DIG-ppmsca-17514.*

The chair of the committee was its oldest member, William Samuel Johnson. He was born in 1727, the son of a leading clergyman. Educated at Yale and Harvard, Johnson had more formal college training than any of the other committee members, and unlike all of them he was deeply religious. He had seen the glory years of the American Empire, had been a colonel in the Connecticut Militia during the French and Indian War, and had served on the colony's Supreme Court from 1771 to 1774. On the eve of the final crisis he had achieved all that a loyal American subject of the crown could have expected. Never formally a loyalist during the fray, he would have preferred peace and reform of the empire to independence. With peace he resumed law practice, though he was more a debt collector than a legal thinker. He served in the confederation Congress from 1785 to 1787. He had learned from hard experience that "wide public acceptance is the test of enduring political achievement." No one, he concluded "whose conduct differs too widely from prevailing public opinion" could ever hold office. Thus he became a quiet trimmer, watching the wind, adjusting his sails, turning the rudder to go with the current.[6]

At first, he was a tepid supporter of the nationalism of Madison and Hamilton. Connecticut public opinion did not favor sweeping constitutional reform. Reluctantly, he accepted his appointment to the Philadelphia Convention. At sixty, he suffered from the heat in the city's late spring and summer (recording in his diary some thirty-three days of "hot" and "very hot"). Cautiously, he spoke at the convention, and much respected for his age and his dignified mien he had great influence. In particular, the southern delegates saw him as an ally. He owned household slaves and probably took one or more with him to Philadelphia, as they did. He was certainly a "gentleman," and his reputation for moderation and compromise helped broker the Great Compromise. Johnson also helped frame Article III, insuring that the U.S. Supreme Court would have equity jurisdiction (the authority to issue injunctions, order the taking of depositions and the like) as well as legal jurisdiction. The High Court's power to frame injunctive relief would in a distant time become the foundation of civil rights decisions like *Brown v. Board of Education*.[7]

## Gouverneur Morris's Handiwork

Johnson presided over the Committee of Style with a light hand. Nothing of his contribution to its deliberations is recorded. Indeed, historians do not know exactly what transpired at the meetings of the Committee of Style. It met in a room above the assembly hall, and its deliberations were not hidden from the other delegates. Though as a member he was present, Madison's notes say nothing of its deliberations.

One fact is certain. At the first meeting, Morris was asked to revise and compress the convention's draft. If he was not Johnson's first choice, Johnson had to acquiesce in the decision. It made sense. Hamilton had proven himself a superb writer, but a fiery one whose temperament was ill suited to close rewriting. He had bemused the assembly with his June 18th speech, and Johnson knew he was a poor choice for the job of redaction of the Committee of Detail's twenty-three clauses. Madison was brilliant but not a particularly able penman. In trying not to give offense his writing could be downright opaque. King was able enough and could have done a fine job, but he would have deferred to his friend and senior colleague Morris. Morris was tireless, Johnson knew, and in all probability wanted and lobbied for the job. Johnson thus assigned the role of rearranging the document to Morris. Late in his life, Morris took credit for the entire work of the Committee of Detail, writing in 1814 to Timothy Pickering, a fellow Federalist, that the Preamble was "written by the fingers which write this letter." Madison confirmed as much when, many years later, he conceded to historical editor Jared Sparks (then working on a collection of George Washington's correspondence), that "with the ready concurrence of the others" Morris had prepared a first draft of the final version. "A better choice [than Morris] could not have been made."[8]

For as much as Madison managed the convention behind the scenes, Morris influenced its deliberations on the State House floor. Though in his many contributions to the debate, more than any other delegate (except Madison), Morris's wit sometimes ran to irony and he was impatient with those who did not see the point of his eloquence, his hauteur was not offensive. Away from the floor of the hall, he was convivial. As a draftsman, he proved himself able to condense and refine the thinking of others. He had already exhibited this skill on the Brearley (Odds and Ends) Committee, writing its report. For this reason alone the Committee of Style may have turned to him. In five days he reduced the twenty-three unwieldy articles given him into the seven articles one finds in the present Constitution—a superb piece of literary craftsmanship.

In all likelihood, Johnson had not asked Morris to rewrite the Preamble, but Morris did. Unlike the preambles in the state constitutions and the preamble to the Articles, Morris's draft had two parts. The first was the address: "We the People of the United States." That term comprised everything for which he had campaigned all spring and summer. It recalled Jefferson's language and the preambles to some of the state constitutions, but he coupled it to a second compelling phrase: "in order to form a more perfect union." "We the People" was incontestably the rephrasing of popular sovereignty, and thus hardly offensive. The sovereign people of a sovereign nation gave this constitution to themselves "and our posterity." By contrast, "We the people of the United States," the nation, rather than the individual states, was a novelty and a deliberate one. The new formulation underlined the premise that the federal government was not a collection of states but a government of and by its people. "In order to establish a more perfect union," following as it did "We the people of the United States," turned union from a confederation into a single nation. By coupling "We the People" to a more perfect union, he indelibly linked the foundation of republicanism—the sovereign people—with the Union.

Make no mistake—Morris abhorred democracy. He did not equate the people as a whole with the mass of individuals. He supported, and lost, a proposal to impose property qualifications for voting in federal elections. He wanted the Senate to reflect the interests of the rich, a counterweight to the political power of the lower orders of men. He knew that the rich would try to corrupt government, for all government demonstrated the inevitable "conflict between the rich and the poor, the few and the many." In this, he was a realist, for these same conflicts continue to roil American politics and political policy-making. But he never was an admirer of aristocracy or plutocracy or any of the forms of government that excluded vibrant and informed popular participation. The people would not "run" the government, but they would select their rulers and could remove them.[9]

Along with "We the People," other phrases in the new Preamble had come from earlier writings—preambles to state constitutions, the Articles of Confederation, the pamphlets and other publications that flooded the intellectual marketplace between 1776 and 1787, and even the correspondence of the delegates. It was Morris's conjunction of the older phraseology, the order in which he arrayed the words, and the small but greatly significant alterations in language he assayed, that made the Preamble into a unique expression of a truly national aspiration.

For example, the Declaration of Independence had a preamble, the work of Thomas Jefferson. Its ringing opening cadences— "When in the course of human events, it becomes necessary for one people to dissolve the political bands which have connected them with another, and to assume among the powers of the earth, the separate and equal station to which the laws of nature and of nature's god entitle them"—contained two references to law, but was not a blueprint for constitutional government. John Dickinson's draft of Articles of Confederation contained the phrases "for their common defense, the security of their liberties, and their mutual and general welfare." Dickinson, like Jefferson and Morris a lawyer, understood that preambles were parts of laws, not mere expressions of opinion, but Morris knew that the Confederation had failed to provide security, defense, and welfare. In 1786, Jefferson returned to the enterprise of drafting preambles with a monstrously long (547 words) and convoluted preface to his Virginia Act for Establishing Religious Freedom (the act itself was only 84 words long). The preamble began crisply enough: "Well aware that Almighty God hath created the mind free; that all attempts to influence it by temporal punishments or burdens, or by civil incapacitations, tend only to beget habits of hypocrisy and meanness," then rambled through every argument Jefferson could conceive against established religions, bigoted churchmen, and superstition, "the impious presumption of legislators and rulers, civil as well as ecclesiastical, who, being themselves but fallible and uninspired men, have assumed dominion over the faith of others, setting up their own opinions and modes of thinking as the only true and infallible, and as such endeavoring to impose them on others."[10]

Nothing in Morris's transformation of common usages into a new and powerful reformulation was accidental. Morris had gone far beyond the task of improving the style and simplifying the arrangement of the draft given the Committee of Style and Arrangement. Morris's preamble was a coup of sorts, and he knew it. How then might he convince the other members of the committee to accede to his bold revision? One can surmise that Hamilton needed no persuading. He was a strong nationalist. King too favored Morris's vision for the new government. Madison must have been wary, but he did not like confrontation, and Morris, Hamilton, and King were like a phalanx with its long spears already lowered. Johnson never made waves when he could avoid it.

Still, Morris cloaked his bold assertion of nationalism in the language that the delegates had already approved—even when he gave the language new force and meaning. For example, he incorporated the terms "common defense" and "general welfare" from the report of the Brearley committee on which he served and whose report he drafted. On September 4, 1787, the committee added that term to what would become Article I, Section 8: "The Congress shall have Power To lay and collect Taxes, Duties, Imposts and Excises, to pay the Debts and provide for the common Defence and general Welfare of the United States; but all Duties, Imposts and Excises shall be uniform throughout the United States." In 1830, Madison would write a long letter giving his own version of the matter (a version discussed in Chapter Five of this book), but no contemporary evidence explains why the delegates added the phrase "and provide for the common defense and general welfare of the United States" to the Taxation Clause. Gouverneur Morris sat on this committee. He was the author of its report to the convention. Thus it was entirely possible that he was the author of the general welfare language in the Taxation Clause as well as the General Welfare Clause in the Preamble. Of course, it is also possible that he liked what someone else in the Committee of Eleven said and adopted it for the Preamble a week later (Madison and King were also members of this "committee of leftovers"), but Morris was more likely to be an instigator rather than a follower when it came to giving the federal government greater powers.[11]

Morris knew that "the common defense" was on everyone's mind at the convention. According to John Jay, the "dangers from foreign arms and influence" worried the revolutionary generation long before the convention met. Divide America into pieces and none of them could afford a navy adequate to protect the extended coast of the Atlantic. Who would pay for such protection, if not a nation? And make no mistake, "certain it is that foreign nations will know and view it exactly as it is, and they will act towards us accordingly." Recognizing the confederation's continued weakness, France had refused to open its West Indian ports to the American trade; the Royal Navy continued to stop American ships and impress American sailors; the Spanish in Florida and along the Mississippi continued to harass American traders; American diplomats in Europe were still slighted—the list went on and on. Divided, the country would be prey to foreign nations' policies of divide and conquer, carrying on their imperial rivalries by pitting one portion of the country against another. "Discord and jealousy" would further divide the country, and the republican experiment would fail. If a foreign nation saw that the United States was "united, they will be much more disposed to cultivate our friendship than provoke our resentment."[12]

Jay did not attend the convention, but he was in contact with Morris, a close friend and political ally. Jay's career spanned the colonial, revolutionary, early national, and the beginning of the Jacksonian eras, during which he was a diplomat in Spain, France, and England, President of the Continental Congress, secretary of foreign affairs during the Confederation period, the first Chief Justice of the United States Supreme Court under the new Constitution, and governor of New York. He opposed slavery more quietly but also more consistently than King and Gouverneur Morris, and was responsible for the New York gradual emancipation act. Moderate, persuasive, neither a democrat nor a reactionary, he was a stalwart of the Federalist Party. He retired from politics in 1801 and lived as a country gentleman until his death in 1829. Described as "reliable, rather than inspirational, solid and admirable without rising to the heroic," Jay had a lawyerly approach to problem solving that made him an obvious choice for diplomatic duties and gave his opinions on the common defense added authority. Morris certainly would have taken Jay's observations, expressed to him privately before Jay published them, seriously.[13]

During the early years of the Revolutionary War in New York, Morris had seen guerilla warfare. Even without Jay's warnings, Morris would have been naturally concerned that the new government make provisions for the common defense. After 1776, Massachusetts was spared the ravages of battle, but Rufus King told the convention on June 19th, the day after Hamilton spoke and departed, that a strong central government was the only safety against "public danger." The common defense was still on his mind on August 28th, when the convention discussed the Committee of Detail report. He worried that a state "might be at liberty" not to defend its attacked neighbor. "Weaknesses" like the importation of slaves into one state might then become weakness of the whole United States.[14]

Pierce Butler of South Carolina also knew about such weaknesses. A cockpit of guerilla raiding throughout the war for Independence, South Carolina had seen its capital, Charleston, fall into British hands after a brutal siege. As well, South Carolina had a black majority that might join with a foreign power should the state be invaded; that very power, in the form of Spanish Florida, was a mere hundred miles away. Georgia was a bulwark against the Spanish menace, but so long as the Spanish offered asylum and liberty to runaway slaves, the threat of slave rebellion could not be dismissed. With Spain entering the war in 1780 on the French side (Spain did not sign a treaty with the United States until the "Treaty of Friendship" in 1795), an uneasy peace had broken out between Spain and the United States, but the war between loyalist and patriot militiamen in the backcountry of the Carolinas continued until 1783. After the war, conflict with the Indian nations on both Carolinas' borders was still a threat. Butler wanted the national government to assume the burdens of the common defense, and on August 18th he suggested that the federal government have the power to call up state militias for the common defense.[15]

No language remained vaguer at the convention than "to promote the general welfare" or "establish justice." While "the people," "liberty," "union," and "defense" had more-or-less fixed denotations in the vocabulary of the framers, "general welfare" did not. Read narrowly, it implied that government should not promote the interests of a few over the interest of the many. Read broadly, however, it seemed to license the federal government to do whatever it needed to do. This was how Hamilton saw the phrase, at least to judge by his later interpretation of it. Morris may simply have borrowed the words from the Articles of Confederation, but by adding them to the Preamble at the front of the federal Constitution, he altered their impact. Placed there they became an injunction to the federal government to *promote* the welfare of *all* the people of the United States. Promoting the welfare of the people required activity, planning, foresight, and energy. These were the very qualities that the Articles of Confederation Congress lacked. Morris wanted a federal government that governed, not one that presided, like a court waiting for cases to come to it, nor let states take the lead.

Although much of the language of the Preamble was common currency when Morris wrote, not every portion of the Preamble echoed in the rest of the Constitution. Common defense and general welfare already appeared in Article I, Section 8, among the purposes for which Congress might raise and spend taxes and other revenues. Domestic tranquility was enforced by the Republican Government Guarantee Clause and the Militia Clause. "Establish justice" was hinted at in Article III, section 1, wherein Congress was given the authority to "ordain and establish inferior courts, and by implication, to assign to them jurisdiction. Congress did that in the Judiciary Act of 1789, one of the first passed when the new government convened. In 1793, the U.S. Supreme Court heard a Georgia challenge to the

Judiciary Act of 1789. That act allowed a citizen of one state to sue another state in federal court, Chisholm, a South Carolina citizen, wanted Georgia to pay for supplies contracted and delivered during the Revolution. Georgia, claiming that it was sovereign, refused to accede to the suit or even to argue its case before the High Court. The Supreme Court, in a divided vote, allowed the suit to go forward. Chief Justice John Jay, one of the four justices in the majority, founded his view of the question on the Preamble to the Constitution. "The people therein declare, that their design in establishing it, comprehended Six objects. 1st. To form a more perfect union. 2d. To establish justice…It would be pleasing and useful to consider and trace the relations which each of these objects bears to the others; and to shew that they collectively comprise every thing requisite, with the blessing of Divine Providence, to render a people prosperous and happy" but it was only necessary to discourse on two of the clauses. "To form a more perfect union" and "to establish justice" were the basis for the provisions of the Judiciary Act in question, a logical and necessary extension of the very purpose of the Preamble, "To controversies between a State and citizens of another State; because in case a State (that is all the citizens of it) has demands against some citizens of another State, it is better that she should prosecute their demands in a national Court, than in a Court of the State to which those citizens belong; the danger of irritation and criminations arising from apprehensions and suspicions of partiality, being thereby obviated."[16]

Jay's attempt to read a strong version of the perfect union language of the Preamble into the Constitution by judicial fiat was not successful at the time. The Eleventh Amendment effectively reversed the High Court's opinion in *Chisholm*, but it was plain that Jay, like Morris, thought that the Preamble was not empty verbiage.

Morris's role in inventing a new Preamble was undoubtedly known to every member of the convention who cared to look. But if anyone missed it, Morris was not one to hide his light under a bushel. The most informed and persuasive explanation of the Committee of Style's choice of phrasing came from the hand that had "written the preamble"—that of Morris himself. On September 12th, he gave to the safekeeping of George Washington a "Draught of the letter from the Convention to Congress, to accompany the Constitution" on its journey to New York City, where the Confederation

Congress awaited it. The letter was not drafted by the committee nor approved by the convention. It was all Morris and thus the surest guide to his thinking.[17]

Morris' draft letter of transmittal began: "We have now the Honor to submit to the Consideration of the United States in Congress assembled that Constitution which has appeared to us the most advisable." Morris offered no hint of the threats of walkout some delegates made, nor of the departure of New York's anti-federalist delegates Lansing and Yates, nor of the long and bitter debates over representation of large states and small states, nor of the quarrels over the powers of the executive and the slave trade. He knew but did not mention Gerry's, Mason's, and Randolph's expressed inclinations not to sign. Instead, Morris wrote, "The Friends of our Country have long seen and desired that the Power of making war Peace and Treaties, that of levying Money & regulating Commerce and the correspondent executive and judicial Authorities should be fully and effectually vested in the general Government of the Union."

Morris continued with a series of miniature essays, each reflecting the ideas of one or another of the members of the Committee of Style. Madison's signal contribution to American constitutional theory—his belief that faction could work in favor of a federal government extended over a vast territory (espoused in Federalist No. 10 two months later)—made a cameo appearance in Morris's letter. How much of his thinking Madison confided to Morris will never be certain. But the similarity between Madison's "Among the numerous advantages promised by a well constructed Union, none deserves to be more accurately developed than its tendency to break and control the violence of faction" and Morris's "The Impropriety of delegating such extensive Trust to one Body of Men is evident. Hence results the Necessity of a different Organization" is certainly intriguing.[18]

A short discourse on the foundations of government followed, in which Morris bowed a little to Hamilton's view of a strong central government and incorporated certain of the ideas in his ill-fated speech to the convention. "Individuals entering into Society must give up a Share of Liberty to preserve the Rest. The Magnitude of the Sacrifice must depend as well on Situation and Circumstances as on the Object to be obtained."

To support that proposition, Morris assayed a brief narrative of the convention, couched in the modest, conciliatory tones that

Johnson favored: "It is at all Times difficult to draw with Precision the Line between those Rights which must be surrendered and those which may be reserved And on the present Occasion this Difficulty was encreased by a Difference among the several States as to their Situation Extent Habits and particular Interests." "Habits and interests" was likely code for slavery, and slavery was the worm in the bud of union, as Morris and King agreed. But, as had Madison and Hamilton at the Convention, Morris skirted the issue and never named the evil.

Morris then turned to the project nearest his own heart—union. "In all our Deliberations on this Subject we kept steadily in our View that which appears to us the greatest Interest of every true American: The Consolidation of our Union." That word—"consolidation"—was anathema to those who feared an all-powerful national government. James Wilson conceded it was "a dread" for those who wanted an undisturbed state sovereignty. Not entirely candidly, for he knew that the various states' delegates would reveal all to the Congress and later to their state's ratification convention, Morris blurred this portion of the work of the convention: "This important Consideration seriously and deeply impressed on our Minds led each State in the Convention to be less rigid on Points of inferior Magnitude than might have been otherwise expected. And thus the Constitution which we now present is the Result of a Spirit of Amity and of that mutual Deference & Concession which the Peculiarity of our political Situation rendered indispensable." But Morris was no Pollyanna. He conceded, "That it will meet the full and entire approbation of every State is not perhaps to be expected."[19]

Did Morris think that the Preamble was "enforceable"? That is, did he think that the portions of the Preamble not reiterated in the body of the Constitution could be the basis for Congressional legislation or for suits in federal courts? He did not address this technical issue. Most later scholarship and judicial decisions presumed that the Preamble to the Constitution, like preambles to statutes, threw light on the purpose of the legislation, but was separate from the enacting formula. To impose this much later view on Morris would be ahistorical and possibly inaccurate. In any case, the dictum that the Preamble was not enforceable was the work of Joseph Story, had no basis in the convention debates, the plain text of the Preamble, or American judicial precedents before Story wrote in 1833.

Morris's letter may have overstated the case because he knew that Lansing and Yates had already departed for New York and were busy denouncing the work of the convention. They had gained the support of the powerful faction around Governor George Clinton. So too Luther Martin and John Francis Mercer of Maryland had bolted and were organizing opposition there. Elbridge Gerry decided not to sign. He wrote to the General Court of Massachusetts on October 18, 1787, that "It was my duty to oppose" the Constitution. He continued, "There is no adequate provision for a representation of the people…the executive is blended with and will have an undue influence over the legislature…the judicial department will be oppressive." His "Objections" to signing would be reprinted by anti-federalist newspapers forty-six times in the coming months. Most worrisome to Morris was the defection of Virginia's Mason and Randolph. Mason decided that he could not sign, and convinced Randolph that the absence of a bill of rights (briefly debated and rejected in mid-August) was a fatal flaw. He too announced his intention not to sign. As Randolph wrote to Madison after they had repaired, respectively, to Richmond and to New York City, "The first raptures in favor of the Constitution were excessive. Every town resounded with applause. The conjectures of my reasons for refusing to sign were extraordinary, and so far malicious as to suppose that I was chagrined at not carrying every point in my own way, or that I sought for popularity." The latter accusation reflected the fact that Patrick Henry and others in Virginia were gearing up to prevent ratification of the Constitution in its present form and had persuaded a weak-willed Randolph to recant his federalism.[20]

## The New Form of Union Defended in Congress

While Morris had no trouble framing his letter in terms of a robust nationalism, the members of the Committee of Style who doubled as state delegates to Congress in New York City—Madison, Johnson, and King—had a more onerous task. They would be the first of the federalists to defend the work of the convention in public. The Congress in which they sat, constituted by the Articles of Confederation, was the very incarnation of state sovereignty (though Article II had a qualification—"each state retains its sovereignty, freedom, and independence, and every power, jurisdiction, and right, which is not by this convention expressly delegated to the United States, in Congress assembled). The express powers comprised the conduct of diplomacy and war, and Indian affairs (but not of Indians who were "members" of any of the states).[21]

In the Congress, after the September 20th reading of the Constitution, Melancton Smith and Robert Lansing of New York, along with Richard Henry Lee of Virginia, all voiced their opposition to sending the Constitution to the states. Lee was openly contemptuous of the proposed frame of federal government. "It cannot be denied, with truth, that this new constitution is, in its first principles, highly and dangerously oligarchic." Indeed, no sooner had the Congress received the new document and its covering materials than Smith, Lansing, and Lee joined forces to defeat the convention's plan to have Congress submit the draft Constitution directly to the states.[22]

How were Johnson, Madison, and King to defend the Preamble, the most far-reaching statement of "We the People" in the draft constitution, before a body filled with future anti-federalists and dedicated to the proposition that each state's sovereignty was inviolate? Among the quietest of the members of the convention, and certainly of the Committee on Style and Arrangement, William Samuel Johnson was clear in his own mind that the Preamble must go to the states as written. When Lee moved to delay sending the Constitution to the states for ratification until the states so instructed the Congress, commonly done when any amendment to the Articles of Confederation was proposed, Johnson sought the floor to speak. He knew that the Articles could not be amended without the unanimous consent of the states. Plainly, Rhode Island, absent from the federal constitutional convention and already opposed to ratification, could then block any move to ratify the Constitution or even launch the ratification process.

Johnson shared his thoughts with Congress on September 26th. Melancton Smith's notes for that day survive. "[Johnson opened] Hardly possible to send it out without approving or disapproving. For this reason, Mr. Lee's motion [ought to be postponed]. Congress ought to approve or disapprove [sending the constitution to the states for ratification]." At best, this was a lukewarm endorsement of the convention's work. Perhaps Johnson, away from Philadelphia's heady nationalism, was again testing the waters. He elected to review events, putting a slight spin on them, showing deference to Congress and to the convention at the same time—Johnson's way of currying favor to achieve his goals. "They [the Congress] may do it. It is their duty to do it." The convention had imposed this duty, contrary to the Articles. The die was cast. "Nothing from Congress would do. The proposal from [the] Convention [is] not a proposal to 9 [states] but to all. It is hoped all will [agree]." One notes Johnson's passive voice, "it is hoped." After all, by sending it to the states, "It don't imply an approbation of all its parts, but the best upon the whole, a matter of accommodation. We say it is better than the present [constitution], better than running the risk of another."[23]

Madison, representing Virginia in Congress, was equally adamant about defeating Lee's motion, but he too expressed his views with diffident modesty. Not only was it Madison's preferred form of speaking, Lee was a friend and a fellow Virginia planter. To offend the powerful Lee clan, particularly in view of Madison's hope to be elected to the federal Congress under the new Constitution, would be political suicide. "The business is open to consideration" Smith's notes on Madison's address began, "[He] should feel delicacy if he had not assented in Convention though he did not approve it." The notes that Melancton Smith took of the rest of Madison's comments are almost impenetrable, because Madison's speeches, like his writings, were full of clauses intricately looped about one another. Madison's habit was to qualify every thing he said, sometimes before he had finished saying it. But the gist of his argument was clear. There was "No probability of Congress agreeing in alterations. Those who disagree, differ in their opinions. A bill of rights [is] unnecessary because the powers are enumerated and only extend to certain cases, and the people who are to agree to it are to establish this." In other words, the constitution had first to be ratified and the new government put into operation before amendments could be proposed.[24]

Finally, Rufus King, the third member of the Committee of Style serving his state in Congress, rose to speak. He had heard enough dilly dallying, and the notes that Smith took had no trouble capturing the Massachusetts' lawyer's sense of urgency. "The House cannot constitutionally make alterations. The idea of [the] Convention originated in the states, and this led the House to agree. They proposed the Convention should propose alterations, which when agreed to here and confirmed by the states [should be adopted], and therefore [Congress] are to agree or disagree to the alterations and cannot alter [the Constitution] consistently with their own act."

King ignored the extent of the "alterations," clearly a lot more fundamental than Congress had in mind that February, and rushed on,
"The majority of the people, it is said [by Richard Henry Lee], may
alter, and if they have manifested a desire to change, this House may
advise it, as it is not obligatory. We may advise as any other body
of men. To satisfy forms it was ordered to pass this House. They
may agree or disagree. If they do disagree it will not prevent them
[the states] to accept. If they [Congress] agree it will give weight."
Congress agreed two days later to send the whole package—the
proposed Constitution, the convention's resolutions, with a letter of
transmittal—to the states' governors for submission to the state legislatures. They, in turn, would provide for elections to ratification
conventions whose members would be chosen by popular ballot.
The people, or at least a portion thereof, would finally speak.[25]

................

After the convention, Morris returned to Morrisiana, now lord of
the domain. He was not certain that the New York State ratifying
convention would agree to the new document. In fact, as he must
have known, the issue was by no means decided. On the eve of the
ratification convention's first session, he wrote to Washington, whose
friendship he claimed from their first meeting at Valley Forge, "With
respect to this state, I am far from being decided in my opinion that
they will consent. True it is, that the city and its neighborhood are
enthusiastic in the cause; but I dread the cold and sour temper of
the back counties, and still more the wicked industry of those who
have long habituated themselves to live on the public, and cannot
bear the idea of being removed from the power and profit of state
government, which has been, and still is, the means of supporting
themselves, their families, and dependents, and (which is perhaps
equally grateful) of depressing and humbling their political adversar-
ies. What opinions prevail more southward, I cannot guess. You are
in a better condition than any other person to judge of a great and
important part of that country."[26]

The Preamble had been his creation. During the days and nights
at Mrs. Dailey's boarding house that second week in September, he
had dared to dream of a great nation whose finest aspirations the
Preamble embodied. Would his countrymen see it, and the rest of
the work of the convention, in the same light?

## CHAPTER 4

# Ratification and the First Federal Administrations, 1787–1801

The federalists of 1787 were a loose coalition dedicated to the ratification of the federal Constitution. The Federalists of the 1790s were a far more disciplined political faction that Alexander Hamilton formed out of the more conservative wing of the federalists. Madison, a leader of the federalists, would become the foremost opponent of the Federalists. At the heart of that distinction was a debate over the implications of the Preamble, for the Federalists of the 1790s saw the constitutional provisions for the general welfare and the common defense as a license to build a strong central government. From that view Madison and what became the Republican Party dissented. But first, the federalists of 1787 had to win the game of ratification.

The federalists were hopeful that the Preamble would help their cause. A month after the conclusion of the convention, John Jay wrote to a correspondent that "a strong sense of the value and blessings of union induced the people, at a very early period, to institute a federal government to preserve and perpetuate it." The working solution was a division of powers, the states retaining their sovereignty rather than becoming departments of the new government. Both governments would have the ability to coerce, raise funds, and manage their own personnel. But the boundary between the two governments, surely a source of friction, was the primary concern of the framers. "The crucial issue of federalism...was rather to decide how the anticipated rivalry of these two levels of government could be resolved short of overt resort to coercion." The series of open-ended phrases of the Preamble left room for a resolution of the competing federal and state governments.[1]

Citing the unremitting dangers of war on the frontiers and coast of the nation, Federalists wrote to one another with confidence that the new Constitution would pass through the ratification process unscathed. But the task of gaining ratification would be no easy feat. Speed and secrecy were on their side, and after some debate so was Congress, but who could predict what would happen when the document arrived at the various states' legislatures? Would they call for ratification conventions or insist on another constitutional convention to amend the document? There might even be violence. No sooner had an express rider brought the instructions from Congress in New York City back to Philadelphia than its federalists rammed approval of the document through the first of the state gatherings. Recalcitrant delegates were roughly handled. Their faces worn and their clothing soiled, sixteen of its members wrote a dismayed address to their constituents. The convention had gone off the track, they warned, and like-minded men in other states must prevent the new government from taking power. Would they?[2]

In the coming months, the anti-federalists would not be silenced. They mounted an intellectual campaign against the Constitution in pamphlets and newspapers essays, and they organized resistance in the state ratification conventions. Their concerns about centralized government and ruling elites, and their concern for personal liberty and bills of rights, have endured as part of the larger story of political dissent within the American public arena.[3]

## Ratification Stories

The story of ratification in the states reminds us of how the Preamble reflected pre-convention experiences. Where the common defense had been imperiled, as in Georgia, whose borders lay open to Spanish incursions and Indian conflict, ratification was quick and relatively painless. Georgia delegates met for one day in Augusta, on December 30, 1787, and voted 26 to 0 to ratify. Delaware voted on December 3rd, and New Jersey on December 18th. Again the balloting was unanimous. The two states, like Georgia, had suffered the terrible depredations of guerilla warfare between loyalist irregulars and state militiamen. The delegates wanted no repeat of the horrors of war fresh in their minds.

In other states, a combination of domestic politics, concern for state autonomy, and desire to see a bill of rights delayed ratification, but the Preamble's promises of a more perfect union and a government that would provide for the general welfare and insure domestic tranquility would win the day. In the two states that were critical to the adoption of the constitution, Virginia and New York, all of these motives came into play.[4]

When the Virginia convention met, on June 24, 1788, Madison knew that his former ally, Edmund Randolph, had switched sides. As well, the redoubtable Patrick Henry and the much respected George Mason would object. Henry was suspicious of central power, and Mason had joined Randolph in refusing to sign the Constitution because it did not contain a bill of rights. Mason wanted a bill of rights much like the ones he had written, in 1776, for the state constitution. Henry was implacably opposed to the Preamble's idea

Patrick Henry.
*Courtesy of the Library of Congress, LC-USZ62-7668.*

of union. "Sir, give me leave to demand, what right had they to say, We the People. My political curiosity, exclusive of my anxious solicitude for the public welfare, leads me to ask who authorized them to speak the language of We the People instead of We the States?"

Henry had made what was, in effect, a fatal admission. Though he did not realize its full implications (no more than later jurists and scholars citing him), he had treated the Preamble as part of the Constitution—not a separate statement of principles or aspirations, but fully a part of the document. For him, it was enforceable. Though he did not credit Morris's authorship, he recognized the implications of Morris's coup, for Morris had wanted an active, consolidated national government and the Preamble provided a basis for such a government. Henry did not want a central government with more power over the people or the states than the confederation exercised, and he rejected the language of the Preamble for that reason.

Mason and Henry spoke well and often of the danger of adopting a constitution without a bill of rights, but Randolph had changed sides again, and with Madison he called for ratification first and amendment later. As Randolph explained, with eight states already having ratified, Virginia's vote would determine "union or no union" and he did not want to be the one blamed for the latter event.

George Wythe agreed with Randolph. He was not a major contributor to debates at the Philadelphia convention. He supported the Constitution there and still did. But he wanted Virginia to instruct the new Congress to amend the Preamble. A much honored law professor at the College of William and Mary whose advocacy of human rights (and abhorrence of slavery) was well known to everyone, Wythe, like Henry and Morris, understood the Preamble to be an enforceable part of the Constitution. George Nicholas responded that the Constitution already had a Preamble and within its ambit lay all of the specific rights Wythe proposed, implying that he too regarded the Preamble as enforceable.

A day later, the federalists knew that victory was within their grasp. On the 26th of June, after three days of remarkably able and learned debate, the convention resolved to send its affirmation of the proposed Constitution to the Congress, along with a resolution—the concession to the dissenters—that the Constitution be soon amended to include basic guarantees of rights, a course Massachusetts and other states had already followed. Madison, unlike Morris, Henry, Wythe, and Nicholas, did not say or imply that the Preamble was enforceable, a silence that would in time become the basis for a very different reading of the Preamble.[5]

At first, New York's ratification convention seemed even less likely to ratify than Virginia's. With the convention meeting in Poughkeepsie, halfway up the Hudson River between Albany and New York City, Governor George Clinton hoped that he and his "friends of the people" from the upstate counties would be safe from the influences of the downstate federalists. The New York convention was poised to be a donnybrook of confederation-era politics—farmers against merchants, the west against the seacoast, democrats against plutocrats. The vote for the delegates was just as divisive and partisan—with the anti-federalists coming from the rural counties and the federalists coming from Long Island, the city of New York, and its immediate environs. The anti-federalists had a clear majority. Robert Yates and John Lansing, the New York delegates who had left the convention before its end were there, as was Clinton. On the other side were Hamilton, Jay, and Robert R. Livingston Jr. Outnumbered but not without some cards of their own to play, the federalists were determined that the game be an even match. The federalists' tactics were simple—keep the debate going until news arrived that a ninth state had ratified.

Hamilton contributed to the strategy with something like a filibuster. Clause by clause, in a magnificent exhibition of lung power and intellectual ability matching his performance at Philadelphia, he addressed every issue. He defended the whole of the Constitution by reference to the Preamble, as he had at the close of his newspaper pieces defending the Constitution on May 28, 1788: "Here, in strictness, the people surrender nothing, and as they retain every thing, they have no need of particular reservations. 'We the people of the United States, to secure the blessings of liberty to ourselves and our posterity, do ordain and establish this constitution for the United States of America.' Here is a better recognition of popular rights than volumes of those aphorisms which make the principal figure in several of our state bills of rights, and which would sound much better in a treatise of ethics than in a constitution of government."[6]

Unlike Madison, with whom he had served on the Committee of Style, Hamilton believed that the Preamble was enforceable, indeed that it was the template for an active federal government. Though it would have been prudent to conceal this view during the ratification debates—so suspicious were the anti-federalists of a strong national government—Hamilton could not help himself. When he found himself the first secretary of the treasury in the federal government, Hamilton would demonstrate just how robustly enforceable he found the Preamble to be.

Each time Hamilton spoke, the leader of the anti-federalist forces, Melancton Smith, felt obligated to answer. "It was not," he said, "his intention to follow that gentleman through all his remarks," then did exactly what he said he would not do. So Hamilton and Smith went at it, back and forth, for a week, until news came on June 24th that Virginia was likely to ratify. The federalists now held a trump card. By early July, with the heat taking its toll, the delegates knew that Virginia and New Hampshire had ratified. Ten states now belonged to the new federal union.[7]

Was New York in or out? It was the same question that Edmund Randolph had asked himself. Hamilton warned of the evils of staying out of the Union, and Jay moved that the Constitution be accepted without conditions. Their praise of the Preamble and its clauses in the Federalist papers (on which more is said in the following pages) was beginning to tell. By the middle of July, Smith, like Randolph, answered the question in the affirmative—New York should ratify. His was the first defection from the anti-federalist camp, and not the last. On July 26th, by a vote of 30 to 27, New York joined the Union.[8]

New York became the eleventh state to ratify. North Carolina, on November 21, 1789, and Rhode Island, on May 29, 1790, ratified, both states entering the Union after the new government had gone into operation. This was hardly the best start to a more perfect union, but at least all the states had joined in the common defense.

## The Federalist

To aid ratification in New York, Hamilton and Jay, both of whom were regulars at the convention, and Madison, who was still serving in the Congress in New York City, met, prepared, and published a series of eighty-five newspaper essays in the city's newspapers between October 27, 1787, and August 16, 1788, with a long break after March 1788 (Madison left for Virginia), resuming in May of the same year. Writing under the pseudonym of Publius—the people's advocate, a reference to an ancient Roman and by implication to the very roots of republicanism—and addressing their ideas "To the People of New York," they surveyed every provision of the new document as well as theories of governance, historical evidence, and the politics of the confederation era. Though not widely disseminated during the period of their composition, the essays were collected and published as a whole at the end of 1788. The authorship of the individual papers was not known for certain until 1944, but now the identification is uncontroversial. The Federalist Papers, as they are now called, are a revered guide to their thinking and a treasury of political thought for that period, as well as a "searching analysis to the enduring and universal problems of every democratic state."[9]

All three authors paid particular attention to the "more perfect union" and "common defense" clauses of the Preamble. Both fit the particular interests of the New York delegates. New York had suffered during the wars with the French and their Canadian Indian allies when other colonies refused to come to its aid. New York's geographical location, between New England and the rest of the country, made it the key to unity. Jay opened the essays with the claim that a "united America" would give fewer "just causes" to provoke foreign aggression than a "disunited America." A united America would give diplomatic status to "the best men," write the most useful treaties, and insure that they were enforced. The "safety" of the people of the entire country would be preserved thereby.[10]

Madison agreed with Jay that the common defense imposed certain duties and afforded a certain license to Congress. As he wrote in Federalist No. 41: "Security against foreign danger is one of the primitive objects of civil society. It is an avowed and essential object of the American Union. The powers requisite for attaining it must be effectually confided to the federal councils.... The answer indeed seems to be so obvious and conclusive as scarcely to justify such a discussion in any place." Madison explained how only a federal government could both provide sufficient forces and control those forces needed to insure national security. "If a federal Constitution could chain the ambition or set bounds to the exertions of all other nations, then indeed might it prudently chain the discretion

John Jay, portrait by Gilbert Stuart.
*Courtesy of the Library of Congress, LC-D416-9856.*

of its own government, and set bounds to the exertions for its own safety."[11]

Hamilton saw the military side of the connection between a more perfect union and the common defense, a natural stance for someone who had spent his young adulthood fighting for the nation's independence. He warned of the "perpetual menacings of danger" surrounding the young nation and contended that its arms had "to be always prepared to repel it." In answer to the anti-federalists' wariness about a federal standing army that could serve as a tyrant's strong arm, Hamilton insisted that the people need not fear. The army would come from the state militias, in effect, from the people themselves. "The power of regulating the militia and of commanding its services in times of insurrection and invasion are natural incidents to the duties of superintending the common defence, and of watching over the internal peace of the confederacy."[12]

## George Washington and the Common Defense

It was understood that George Washington would be the first president of the United States, and the college of electors obeyed this unwritten command. When the new federal Congress assembled, Washington sent it what would become the first presidential "Message to Congress," on January 8, 1790. Washington focused on the more perfect union and the common defense. "Among the many interesting objects which will engage your attention that of providing for the common defense will merit particular regard. To be prepared for war is one of the most effectual means of preserving peace." Washington's experience at Valley Forge had left an indelible mark on him. He urged Congress to provide the means to defend the country—the sword and shield—should he need to wield them as commander in chief under the Constitution. "A free people ought not only to be armed, but disciplined…and their safety and interest require that they should promote such manufactories as tend to render them independent of others for essential, particularly military, supplies." He recalled with dismay how American diplomats went scrounging for European ordnance and funding during the Revolutionary War.[13]

But Jay's considerations, Madison's logic, and Hamilton's confidence, even with Washington's plea added, did not stop other imperial powers from involving the United States in their contests. The Preamble's promise of a common defense should have signaled national unity in the face of these threats. Instead, President Washington encountered internal divisions arising from external threats. The implications of war in Europe came to American shores when, in 1792, hostilities erupted between Britain and Revolutionary French Republic. The French actively sought U.S. support, sending

Edmond Genet as an emissary to America to raise southern volunteers for the European war. Washington, believing in the futility of taking sides in a European war, officially declared the U.S. neutral. "The duty and interest of the United States require, that they should with sincerity and good faith adopt and pursue a conduct friendly and impartial toward the belligerent Powers." He knew that this was not likely, as some Americans still regarded Britain as the enemy while others were terrified of the disorders the French Revolution had unleashed. "I have therefore thought fit...to exhort and warn the citizens of the United States carefully to avoid all acts and proceedings whatsoever, which may in any manner tend to contravene such disposition." Unable to do more with the forces at his disposal, Washington concluded that the best common defense was to avoid antagonizing any of the warring parties.[14]

Washington did not fear American vessels would violate wartime waters or that American merchants might make windfall profits trading with the combatants as much as he feared that domestic partisanship over the war would undermine the common defense. As he told the nation in his Farewell Address, a good portion of which Hamilton had either revised or written based in part on his own contributions to the Federalist, "All obstructions to the execution of the laws, all combinations and associations, under whatever plausible character, with the real design to direct, control, counteract, or awe the regular deliberation and action of the constituted authorities, are destructive of this fundamental principle, and of fatal tendency. They serve to organize faction, to give it an artificial and extraordinary force."[15]

## Alexander Hamilton and the General Welfare

Washington's Secretary of the Treasury, Alexander Hamilton, saw in the General Welfare Clause a basis for an active domestic policy. In practice, government among the English-speaking peoples during the eighteenth century had limited aims. It was generally understood that at a minimum states protected their territory, collected taxes, and promoted the interests of the official religion of the state. To these purposes the American Revolution had added the concept of rights. As historian Carl Becker described it during World War II, a war fought against tyrants who despised human rights, "The liberal democratic revolution of the eighteenth century was directed against a social system in which political power was excessive, arbitrary, and concentrated. The founding fathers were therefore predisposed, both by political experience and the political philosophy they embraced, to regard political power as inherently dangerous." Thus they posed their provisions of rights as statements of negative law rather than of positive law—limits on how far government could intrude into everyday life.[16]

But the conventional political theory was misleading. In fact, eighteenth-century governments did thrust themselves into everyday life. They set prices and wages, provided poor houses and workhouses for the needy, forced servants and slaves to remain in their bonds, and granted such privileges as monopolies. Governments adopted social control measures, for example ordinances against profaning the Sabbath and drinking in public. Criminal law punished more serious violations of private rights and public order. Civil law regulated the conduct of private citizens toward one another. The general welfare depended on laws that were, in the elevated language of the French "Declaration of the Rights of Men and of Citizens" (1789), "the expression of the general will" in which "All citizens have the right to take part personally, or by their representatives, [in] its formation. It must be the same for all, whether it protects or punishes."[17]

In a more theoretical way, the general welfare connoted the needs of the commonwealth, a collective obligation. Citizens were to put the interests of the whole ahead of their personal interests, another way of expressing the ideal of "civic virtue" that underlay John Adams's notion of the blessings of liberty. It was "devotion to the commonweal," even to the sacrifice of one's private interest. Even so, men who praised the ideal of disinterested public service were at the same time eager solicitors for the patronage of those in power and when they themselves gained office, they dispersed the spoils of victory to their followers.[18]

In 1790, Hamilton opened a controversy over the breadth of the federal government's general welfare powers. Faced with a staggering national debt and sagging creditor confidence, Hamilton viewed the General Welfare Clause of Article I in light of the nearby Necessary and Proper Clause (Article I, Section 8, clause 18: "The Congress shall have Power - To make all Laws which shall be necessary and proper for carrying into Execution the foregoing Powers, and all other Powers vested by this Constitution in the Government of the United States, or in any Department or Officer thereof"). His plans to fund and assume the debts of the states passed Congress, and his agents were already selling the new bonds in Europe. His plan to create a national bank had been approved, to be sure at the cost of agreeing to move the national capital from Philadelphia to a site on the banks of the Potomac River. These bold steps constituted what his enemies derisively called a "loose interpretation" of the Constitution. In light of the Preamble, however, they simply gave force to the promise of legislation for the general welfare.

As he defended his next proposal, a program to award bounties to manufacturers, in a 1791 message to Congress, he conceded, "A Question has been made concerning the Constitutional right of the Government of the United States to apply this species of encouragement, but there is certainly no good foundation for such a question. The National Legislature has express authority 'To lay and Collect taxes, duties, imposts and excises, to pay the debts and provide for the Common defence and general welfare.'" Uniformity of the taxes imposed was the only condition that his reading of the Taxation Clause required of the proposed legislation.[19]

Taxes collected from the general public and used to encourage particular enterprises did not seem uniform, but Hamilton had an answer to that, too. "The power to raise money is plenary, and indefinite; and the objects to which it may be appropriated are no less comprehensive, than the payment of the public debts and the providing for the common defence and 'General Welfare.'" If, in the opinion of the majority of both houses of Congress the disbursement of federal revenue need not be uniform, nor a repayment of debts, then there could be no constitutional objection to it. "The terms 'General Welfare' were doubtless intended to signify more than was expressed or imported in those which Preceded; otherwise numerous exigencies incident to the affairs of a Nation would have been left without a provision." This, of course, was what advocates of limited federal government wanted—no provision for Congress to decide which exigencies merited special-interest legislation. Hamilton hid behind a tautology. "The phrase is as comprehensive as any that could have been used; because it was not fit that the constitutional authority of the Union, to appropriate its revenues shou'd have been restricted within narrower limits than the 'General Welfare' and because this necessarily embraces a vast variety of particulars, which are susceptible neither of specification nor of definition." In short, Hamilton wanted to read the general welfare clause in Article I in light of the General Welfare Clause of the Preamble.

Hamilton's "Report on Manufactures," with its bounties, was a bridge too far for Hamilton's party in Congress to cross. It failed of passage. Madison and others in Congress denounced it as a class measure. Perhaps more important, they saw it as a license for Congress to exercise powers in the name of general welfare nowhere else enumerated in Article I. As Madison had written in Federalist No. 41 three years earlier, "Some, who have not denied the necessity of the power of taxation, have grounded a very fierce attack against the Constitution, on the language in which it is defined." At the time he wrote this newspaper essay, Madison was trying to answer the anti-federalists' complaint "that the power 'to lay and collect taxes, duties, imposts, and excises, to pay the debts, and provide for the common defense and general welfare of the United States,' amounts to an unlimited commission to exercise every power which may be alleged to be necessary for the common defense or general welfare." He thought that such fears of the General Welfare Clause—the Preamble version of the power—were misguided. No one would try to extend federal power that far.[20]

Hamilton had achieved what Madison could not have foreseen when they worked together on the Committee of Style. Hamilton had managed to fuse the two references to the general welfare into one. By broadening the scope of general welfare in his reading of Article I, Hamilton imported into the narrow confines of the taxation power the unlimited implications of the Preamble. General welfare in the latter had no bounds. If the general welfare language of the Taxation Clause could be read in light of the general welfare language of the Preamble, the former would also have no bounds.

Madison had not seen this coming. In all sincerity he had written during the ratification debates "but what color can the objection have, when a specification of the objects alluded to by these general terms immediately follows?" Surely general welfare was defined by the terms of Article I, Section 8, not by the open-ended language of the Preamble. "Nothing is more natural nor common than first to use a general phrase, and then to explain and qualify it by a recital of particulars," he supposed. The breadth of the general welfare in the Preamble must be narrowed by the enumeration of powers in Article I.[21]

Who was the apostate, Hamilton or Madison? Did the federalism of the 1787–1788 years naturally flow into the Federalism of Hamilton? Or was Hamilton's loose construction of the Preamble, among other parts of the Constitution, a violation of the trust placed in him by Madison and other "strict constructionists"? Certainly Hamilton had such an interpretation in mind when he served on the Committee of Style, unless he had changed his mind after his June 18th oration. He had that interpretation in mind when he pressed for ratification in New York. He brought that interpretation with him when he joined Washington's first cabinet. If Madison though that the Constitution as written (as opposed to how Hamilton would have written it) would prevent Hamilton from overreaching when the two collaborated on the Federalist papers, the Virginian was naive—or himself inconsistent.[22]

In 1791, Madison's elder alter ego, Thomas Jefferson, then Secretary of State, accused Hamilton of breaking trust with the federalists. It was an ironic accusation, for Jefferson had verged on anti-federalism in 1787. By 1791, however, Jefferson was a federal official. Expounding on the limits on the General Welfare Clause in Article I in a letter to George Washington, Jefferson condemned Hamilton's reading of the powers of Congress. "[T]he laying of taxes is the power, and the general welfare the purpose for which the power is to be exercised. They [Congress] are not to lay taxes ad libitum [ad lib—at one's discretion, or on the spot] for any purpose they please; but only to pay the debts or provide for the welfare of the Union." Hamilton wanted to use public money to promote private enterprise. He saw it as promoting the economy as a whole, hence a form of general welfare. Jefferson saw it as paying off Hamilton's friends with public funds, the very sort of corruption he and others (including Hamilton) decried during the Revolutionary crisis.[23]

## The Problem of Domestic Tranquility, Again

The Preamble's command to establish justice echoed in Congress's decision to establish a system of federal courts (the Constitution's Article III only described the Supreme Court), as Jay opined in

*Chisholm.* The jurisdiction of these "inferior" courts included disputes over title to lands in the national domain (the territory ceded to the national government by the states in the 1780s). Land was the greatest potential source of wealth in the new nation and land speculation its leading industry. Who might sell it; who might buy it; who might own it? The contest for dominion, for control of land and wealth, always bred corruption from the top of society down to its least powerful members.

With the vast western lands acquired in the Treaty of 1783 ending the War for Independence, the traditions of rough justice that marked the Indian wars of the revolutionary period carried over into the formative years of the new nation. Without their French and British allies to protect them, Indian cultivators were forcibly dispossessed by land-hungry American farmers and unscrupulous land speculators, aided and abetted by the federal courts.

In 1790, President Washington addressed the domestic violence on the frontier in his second annual message. He regarded the western settlements as part of the American political family and saw the Indians who violated the peace as common criminals. "It has been heretofore known to Congress that frequent incursion have been made on our frontier settlements by certain banditti of Indians from the northwest side of the Ohio. These, with some of the tribes dwelling on and near the Wabash, have of late been particularly active in their depredations, and being emboldened by the impunity of their crimes…they have, instead of listening to the humane invitations and overtures made on the part of the United States, renewed their violences with fresh alacrity and greater effect." The Indians resented the theft of their hunting grounds and fields and returned blow for blow, but to Washington and others in the new federal government, Indian "self-help" to recover ancestral lands was domestic violence. He felt the same way about his domestic help, selling away any slave who misbehaved or disobeyed him. By contrast, to those who treated him as a benevolent master he returned kindness and care.[24]

Washington based his Indian policy on the Domestic Tranquility Clause of the Preamble and his duties under it. "These aggravated provocations rendered it essential to the safety of the Western settlements that the aggressors should be made sensible that the Government of the Union is not less capable of punishing their crimes than it is disposed to respect their rights and reward

George Washington, by Edward Savage, 1793.
*Courtesy of the Library of Congress, LC-DIG-ppmsca-15711.*

their attachments." If the Indians had obeyed their white father in Philadelphia, domestic tranquility could be restored. Their docility, like the duty a child owed its parents, would be rewarded. "As this object could not be affected by defensive measures, it became necessary to put in force the act which empowers the President to call out the militia for the protection of the frontiers." Necessity, not choice, impelled Washington to "authorize an expedition in which the regular troops in that quarter are combined with such drafts of militia as were deemed sufficient." A stern father with a disobedient child would do no less.[25]

At the time, he told Congress, "The event of the measure is yet unknown to me. The Secretary of War is directed to lay before you a statement of the information on which it is founded, as well as an estimate of the expense with which it will be attended." Washington had ordered General Arthur St. Clair, the governor of the Northwest Territory and the senior American officer at the time, to guard the settlements and quell the disturbances. His ill-prepared force was mauled at the battle of the Wabash. The result was a stand-off between Washington and angry members of Congress. (They demanded to see the correspondence with St. Clair, Washington refused, and the first "executive privilege" contest was won by the president.)

The status of Indians within the federal lands continued to trouble the federal government and bedevil the native peoples well into recent history. The special relationship between the Indian peoples and the government rested upon treaties, suggesting that Indian tribes (itself a legalistic invention not of Indian origin) were sovereign foreign nations, but a series of judicial and executive decisions suggested something quite different, that Indians occupied a unique place in American law—"domestic, dependent nations" according to Chief Justice John Marshall in *Cherokee Nation v. Georgia* (1831). This circumlocution allowed the federal government to regulate Indian affairs, move Indian peoples onto reservations, and otherwise intrude into Indian lives in a way that the government did not intervene in foreign affairs.[26]

In an ironic way, then, the Domestic Tranquility Clause of the Preamble, rather than the treaty-making clauses of the body of the Constitution, became the basis of early national Indian policy, a foundation on which the singular effect given treaties and the unique aspects of federal Indian policy rested. As the Act of 1800 "For the Preservation of Peace with the Indian Tribes" related, any act "to disturb the peace and tranquillity of the United States" by the Indians or those who dealt with them was a federal offense. Although abrogation of treaties with foreign powers is not unknown in American history (in 1800, for example, the United States unilaterally abrogated the 1778 Treaty which brought French aid and French arms to the service of the American revolutionaries), no set of treaties was more often and more cynically abrogated or ignored than those with Indian tribes. Tribes were self-governing, except when they were not. "An Indian tribe in the United States is still recognized by the United States Supreme Court as a distinct, independent, political body possessing all the powers of self-government of any sovereignty, except insofar as those powers have been extinguished." In short, domestic tranquility was almost infinitely malleable when it came to native peoples, and the law accommodated shifts in policy.[27]

Within the western sections of the new states, major domestic insurrections also tested Washington's conception of the Domestic Tranquility Clause. A series of federal excise taxes in 1791 and 1792 on distilled spirits that Secretary of the Treasury Alexander Hamilton proposed to pay off the federal debt gave rise to resistance in Pennsylvania's farming communities, where grains that were not sold or turned into flour were made into spirits. Farmers were required to pay the taxes if they sold these alcoholic spirits. Tax collectors sent from the capital in Philadelphia to collect the taxes were attacked. Washington informed Congress of his planned response in his Fourth Annual Message: "The prosperous state of our revenue has been intimated. This would be still more the case were it not for the impediments which in some places continue to embarrass the collection of the duties on spirits distilled within the United States. These impediments have lessened and are lessening in local extent, and, as applied to the community at large, the contentment with the law appears to be progressive." Again the analogy was to the domestic condition, wherein localities were parts of a larger polity. "But symptoms of increased opposition having lately manifested themselves in certain quarters, I judged a special interposition on my part proper and advisable." The stern father had once more to intervene to insure domestic harmony. "Under this impression [I] have issued a proclamation warning against all unlawful combinations and proceedings having for their object or tending to obstruct the operation of the law in question, and announcing that all lawful ways and means would be strictly put in execution for bringing to justice the infractors thereof and securing obedience thereto."

Washington had never studied law, but he understood his duties under Article II of the Constitution and had at his side Hamilton to remind him of his powers. "Measures have also been taken for the prosecution of offenders, and Congress may be assured that nothing within constitutional and legal limits which may depend upon me shall be wanting to assert and maintain the just authority of the laws." But western Pennsylvania was not easily mollified, and sterner actions were required.[28]

On August 11, 1794, Washington read the riot act to the resisters. "It is in my judgment necessary under the circumstances of the case to take measures for calling forth the militia in order to suppress the combinations aforesaid, and to cause the laws to be duly executed; and I have accordingly determined so to do." Though most of his adult life was spent in uniform, Washington was not acting as the great man on horseback. Instead, he was a bereaved father, "feeling the deepest regret for the occasion, but withal the most solemn conviction that the essential interests of the Union demand it." Washington believed the danger to extend beyond the perpetrators to their sympathizers, hinting that he (and Hamilton, who had a good deal to do with the drafting of the proclamation) knew that the excise tax was widely unpopular. "And I do moreover warn all persons whomsoever against aiding, abetting, or comforting the perpetrators of the aforesaid treasonable acts." Washington did not state in the proclamation the explicit legal authority for his actions. He did not impose martial law and he did not regard the insurrection as a state of national emergency. Instead, he regarded it as a domestic disorder.

Washington's desire to act within the confines of his constitutional powers bespoke a commitment to the aims of the convention that he had chaired. He sought advice from cabinet members, worked closely with the judiciary, and reported his actions to Congress. "An associate justice of the Supreme Court of the United States [riding circuit in western Pennsylvania] notified to me that 'in the counties of Washington and Allegheny, in Pennsylvania, laws of the United States were opposed, and the execution thereof obstructed, by combinations too powerful to be suppressed by the ordinary course of judicial proceedings or by the powers vested in the marshal of that district.'" As president of the United States, he "sought and weighted what might best subdue the crisis." The determination of grounds for calling out the militia thus did not rest on Congress or, initially, on the president, but on the finding of a judge. "On the one hand the judiciary was pronounced to be stripped of its capacity to enforce the laws; crimes which reached the very existence of social order were perpetrated without control; the friends of Government were insulted, abused, and overawed into silence or an apparent acquiescence." There was disorder in the house, "and to yield to the treasonable fury of so small a portion of the United States would be to violate the fundamental principle of our Constitution," that is, the Domestic Tranquility Clause of the Preamble.

Still Washington hesitated to intervene, for "to array citizen against citizen, to publish the dishonor of such excesses, to encounter the expense and other embarrassments of so distant an expedition, were steps too delicate, too closely interwoven with many affecting considerations, to be lightly adopted." The Constitution posed checks on precipitate behavior. Congress was not in session, and there was no threat to public order outside of western Pennsylvania and a small portion of western Maryland. "I postponed, therefore, the summoning of the militia immediately into the field, but I required them to be held in readiness." When the federal troops entered the area, no fighting ensued, the ringleaders were arrested, and after their conviction at trial on charges of treason, Washington pardoned them. He had seen over a long military career the effects of real violence, and had no desire to add to it. What is more, "he knew the western country," the temper of its people, the hardships they faced, and he wished no "insult" to them.[29]

The tax resisters of 1794 argued that they spoke for the people, the same defense as the followers of Daniel Shays had claimed for their actions. Both bodies of men insisted that they acted to preserve the blessings of liberty, a blessing that all free men might claim. "It was the very principles of the Revolution, as they understood them, that the whiskey rebels so lustily espoused." But the Preamble had guaranteed federal intervention in state affairs when domestic tranquility was at stake. In this sense, the Preamble's clauses seemed to be at war with one another, but one might expect that such broad language as the framers of the Preamble crafted might have within it many potential contradictions.[30]

## The Preamble and the War Scare of 1798–1800

Washington's policy of neutrality and his desire to avoid entangling alliances that would bring Europe's wars to American shores did not stop the British governor-general of Canada from telling a council of Indians to destroy American settlements in the Northwest, nor did it prevent the Royal Navy from seizing over 250 American ships bound for France late in 1793. The Republicans invoked these assaults on American sovereignty and honor to urge that the nation declare war on Britain. In 1794, seeking to protect American interests and prevent a rupture with Britain, Washington sent U.S. Supreme Court Chief Justice John Jay to Britain to negotiate a treaty. The resulting treaty disappointed Washington and, when they learned its terms, infuriated the Republicans. The British promised to withdraw their troops from American soil and to open West Indian markets, but said nothing about America's neutral ships on the seas. Worse, the British continued to "impress" (seize) American sailors from American flag ships and force the sailors (allegedly deserters from the Royal Navy) to serve on British ships. The Federalists had a majority in the Senate and ratified the treaty in 1795. In the House, the Republicans at first threatened to hold up the appropriation (payment) necessary for carrying the treaty into effect, but finally acquiesced. In the streets, however, Republicans paraded effigies of "that damn'ed arch-traitor, Jay."[31]

The nation was ill equipped to wage war. With a tiny standing army (revolutionary thinkers agreed that a standing army was the surest path to tyranny in a republic), a small navy (during the war the U.S. had relied on privateers—merchant ships armed with cannon sailing under a letter from the Congress permitting the seizing of enemy shipping), and a huge coastline and frontier to protect, the United States could not have done otherwise than it did—staying out of the European conflict. But France's new government (a conservative Directory had replaced the radical estates general) regarded the Jay Treaty as an insult. The French began seizing American ships carrying goods to Britain, and had by 1798 taken more than three hundred vessels.

Like Washington, newly elected president John Adams did not want war and sent a diplomatic mission to France to negotiate a settlement. The French allowed three private citizens (called X, Y, and Z in the correspondence) to solicit a bribe before the French would meet with Adams's delegation—Charles Cotesworth Pinckney, Elbridge Gerry, and John Marshall. The first two men had been delegates to the Constitutional Convention. Marshall, a Federalist lawyer and member of Congress from Virginia, was younger than Pinckney and Gerry, but Adams saw greatness in Marshall and already trusted him. The delegation reported the "XYZ Affair" to the Federalist newspapers, and they began to demand war. "Millions for defense, but not one cent for tribute" was their slogan, coined by Federalist Congressman Robert Goodloe Harper of South Carolina but widely attributed to Pinckney. American privateers began a "quasi-war" (undeclared conflict) on French cargo ships in the Caribbean.[32]

Congress also voted to establish a large army with Washington at its head and Hamilton as its second in command. But Adams did not trust Hamilton and was disgusted at the way that Hamilton was pulling strings behind his back. Adams's own sense of right and wrong intervened to prevent war. In 1799, over other Federalists' objections, he sent a second mission to France, led this time by Chief Justice Oliver Ellsworth and Marshall. The new mission settled most of the outstanding disputes and averted war.[33]

In the interim a diplomatic crisis became a constitutional crisis. The Federalists in Congress passed and John Adams, somewhat reluctantly, signed an act penalizing seditious libel (criticism of the government), a new naturalization act (raising the period for naturalization from five to fourteen years), an Enemy Aliens Act, and an Alien Friends Act (both giving the president the power to expel aliens), all allegedly designed to protect the country from internal enemies. The Federalists found a justification in the Preamble to the Constitution for their legislative agenda—they acted in the common defense.

The power to expel aliens and suppress dissent in time of war, or looming war, was very deeply embedded in English constitutional history and reappeared in American revolutionary history. Madison himself had expressed concern before, during, and after the Constitutional Convention that aliens posed a dangerous factionalism. Adams always saw the acts as necessary for the approaching war. First Lady Abigail Adams welcomed them, and may have influenced the president to sign them. In the congressional debates over the acts, Federalists repeatedly cited the common defense. Out of doors, Federalists made the same argument. Charles Lee, for example, a Virginia Federalist, and a former U.S. attorney general under Washington and Adams, asked "would it have been prudent or safe, under these circumstances to have been without a law that authorized the removal of aliens dangerous to the peace and safety of the United States"? Opponents of the laws in Congress called them unconstitutional, but the Federalists replied that no government could provide for the common defense if it could not determine who might stay within its borders.[34]

The Sedition Act was the most sweeping of the four pieces of legislation, and it applied to anyone who "shall unlawfully combine or conspire together, with intent to oppose any measure or measures of the government of the United States...or to impede the operation of any law of the United States, or to intimidate or prevent any person holding a place or office in or under the government of the United States, from undertaking, performing or executing his trust or duty." The act also penalized "any person [who] shall write, print, utter or publish, or shall cause or procure to be written, printed, uttered or published, or shall knowingly and willingly assist or aid in writing, printing, uttering or publishing any false, scandalous and malicious writing or writings against the government of the United States" or any of its officers, including the president, his cabinet, and the federal judges. Given that these were all Federalists, the act was clearly designed to suppress the Republican Party on the eve of the 1800 election. Federal prosecutors immediately busied themselves bringing indictments in grand juries handpicked by Federalist marshals, for trial before Federalist jurors (again handpicked) presided over by Federalist judges. The Republicans were justly furious.[35]

Discussing the problems of opposing the Federalists' legislative initiative with Thomas Jefferson when the two men met after Congress had adjourned, Madison realized that one way to safely formulate and espouse a constitutional argument against the Federalists' invocation of common defense was to have it promulgated by the state legislature of Virginia. Jefferson had already seized upon this plan and was drafting a set of "Resolves" for consideration of the Kentucky legislature. These he secretly gave to John Breckinridge, a friend and fellow Republican. Breckinridge then passed them on to Wilson Cary Nicholas to lay before the Kentucky legislature. Kentucky adopted them on November 12, 1798.

Jefferson's draft resolutions rejected the Federalists' loose construction of the Preamble. He insisted "That the several States composing the United States of America, are not united on the principle of unlimited submission to their General Government; but that, by a compact under the style and title of a Constitution for the United States, and of amendments thereto, they constituted a General Government for special purposes." Later thinkers with different purposes would expand this notion into "states' rights," the theory that the Constitution bound together sovereign states by their own consent, and the federal government could only exercise those powers "delegated" to it explicitly in the Constitution. All other powers were reserved to the states. "Whensoever the General Government assumes undelegated powers, its acts are unauthoritative, void, and of no force." This was the doctrine of Nullification, and it too would gain a shape and momentum that would have horrified the federalists of 1787 (as it did Madison many years later).[36]

Madison knew that Jefferson had authored the Kentucky legislation. He must have winced when he read Jefferson's view of the more perfect union as a "compact" of the states. That was not what the Preamble said, nor what Madison had written in his Federalist essays. In the closing weeks of 1798 Madison wrote a set of resolutions for the Virginia House of Delegates (later called the "Virginia Resolves") that dismissed the "common defense" justification for the acts. One might regard such steps as upsetting the "exact balance or equipoise" between federal and state sovereignty that Madison had so carefully constructed in Federalist No. 10 and reiterated on the floor of the House of Representatives in 1791, but in 1798 he thought the danger to republican government so great that more drastic measures—or at least more drastic words—were needed.[37]

Jefferson's resolves went to Kentucky anonymously, and his authorship was not revealed for many years. Madison's authorship of the Virginia Resolves was common knowledge. Madison was no longer a member of the Virginia House of Delegates (one of the great achievements of the revolutionaries was ridding the law of multiple office holding), but his views commanded the respect of the majority of the assembly. Working at a fevered pace in his boarding house room in Richmond, he drafted a resolution for the body which at first sounded like Madison the nationalist of September 1787: "Resolved, that the General Assembly of Virginia, doth unequivocally express a firm resolution to maintain and defend the Constitution of the United States, and the Constitution of this State, against every aggression either foreign or domestic, and that they will support the government of the United States in all measures warranted by the former." He was as committed to the common defense in 1798 as he had been in 1787. That commitment was part of his federalist principles. He pledged Virginia to those principles: "That this assembly most solemnly declares a warm attachment to the Union of the States, to maintain which it pledges all its powers." But Virginia was part of a Union of the states, not a union of the people. This hinted at a slide toward a states'-rights reading of the Constitution. In states'- rights ideology, the states not only retain their sovereignty within the federal system, they can assert their sovereignty against the federal government. "For this end, it is their duty to watch over and oppose every infraction of those principles which constitute the only basis of that Union." The United States was not at war in 1798. Although "there is not a single power whatever that may not have some reference to the common defense," the Federalists' preparations for war, including close scrutiny of alien residents and the enlisting of an army and the commissioning of officers for that army, required the concurrence of the states, for the common defense was one of "the powers of the federal government, as resulting from the compact, to which the states are parties."[38]

Madison's draft was not entirely inconsistent with his defense of the federal principle in the Federalist papers. In Federalist No. 39 he had tried to allay fears that the federal government would crush the states. Ratification "is to be given by the people, not as individuals composing one entire nation; but as composing the distinct and independent States to which they respectively belong. It is to be the assent and ratification of the several States" that will give rise to the federal government. In Federalist No. 46 he again put to rest fears that the states were powerless against the federal government. "Many considerations, besides those suggested on a former occasion, seem to place it beyond doubt that the first and most natural attachment of the people will be to the governments of their respective States...should an unwarrantable measure of the federal government be unpopular in particular States, which would seldom fail to be the case, or even a warrantable measure be so, which may sometimes be the case, the means of opposition to it are powerful and at hand." The means were those that Madison now sought to employ.[39]

But the Preamble had not made the states "parties" to the federal government. Nowhere in the Constitution was there a basis for the compact theory of the Union. Madison had sailed into uncharted waters. He continued that the "compact" did not authorize the federal government to go beyond the "the grants enumerated in that compact." One of those "grants" (a term suggesting that the states rather than the people were the component parts of the Union) was the common defense. The Constitution that Virginia had ratified in 1788 barred states from declaring war or carrying on the diplomacy that might avert or end wars. The common defense was an enumerated and thus exclusively federal power. But Madison asked Virginia to "solemnly appeal to the like dispositions of the other states, in confidence that they will concur with this commonwealth." Asking states to determine in effect what required and what did not require steps in the common defense was exactly what the authors of the Federalist papers denounced.

Although the Virginia lower house adopted the draft, 100 to 63, and on December 24, 1798, Virginia transmitted the resolves to the other states, one must not lose sight of the fact that the Federalists' claims of common defense were not without constitutional basis, even if they acted precipitously on this occasion. From his home at Mount Vernon, Washington repeatedly wrote to Adams that strong measures must be taken to keep the nation safe from internal as well as external enemies. The "arts" of deception of the French, "and those of their agents [in America] to countenance and invigorate opposition" required strong countermeasures. The Federalists' fear of the influence of French radicalism was unfounded. Their fear of the democratic tendencies of the Republicans was unrealistic. Their fear of public opposition to their policies violated the spirit of the Bill of Rights. But their legislative enactments and their prosecution of anti-war sentiment in the courts was a harbinger of similar enactments and prosecutions during the Civil War, World War I, and World War II.[40]

Madison had a hand in writing the Common Defense Clause into both the Preamble and the taxation provisions of Article I. He served on both the Brearley committee and the Committee on Style. The Virginia Resolution's dismissal of those lines in the Constitution read awkwardly at best and hypocritically at worst. Madison had second thoughts almost immediately. Re-reading the resolves, he must have seen the obvious contradictions between it and his earlier views of the common defense. On January 7, 1800, the Virginia assembly issued a report that Madison drafted (he was elected to the state legislature in 1799). In it, he shifted from a states'-rights basis for his argument against the acts to a strict construction argument. This deflected a charge of inconsistency on his part and signified a return to the Madison of the Federalist No. 39: "Whenever, therefore, a question arises concerning the constitutionality of a particular power, the first question is, whether the power be expressed in the Constitution. If it be, the question is decided. If it be not expressed the next inquiry must be, whether it is properly an incident to an express power, and necessary to its execution. If it be, it may be exercised by Congress. If it be not, Congress cannot exercise it."[41]

Had the federal government possessed indefinitely extendable powers, there would have been no need for "necessary and proper" language. He thus turned the Federalist argument for common defense on its head. It was not an open-ended invitation to shout "war" and go beyond the precise strictures of the Constitution. The clause proved the limited character of the national government, not its infinite extension. During the debates in the Virginia ratification convention in 1788, "it was invariably urged" by Madison, among others, "to be a fundamental and characteristic principle of the Constitution, that all powers not given by it were reserved; that no powers were given beyond those enumerated in the Constitution."

Madison saw in the Federalists' reading of the Preamble the dangers of a federal tyranny against which state sovereignty was one bulwark. He would refine this stance in the years to come. A series of constitutional quarrels tested that view of the Preamble, and to Madison's aid would come the most learned and most respected jurist of the middle period of American history—Joseph Story. But neither Madison's cautions nor Story's compromises could prevent the onset of the most critical test of the Constitution: southern secession. In the face of it, Abraham Lincoln would assay a very different interpretation of the Preamble.

.........................

## CHAPTER 5

# The Preamble in Crisis Times, 1801–1865

In the years between the triumph of the Jeffersonian party and the Civil War, the meaning and application of the Preamble became a partisan issue. Views on it were more extreme than those expressed in the formative years of the new federal government. For "We the People" confronted an increasingly dangerous fact: The Union was coming asunder, splitting into antagonistic free- and slave-state sections. The Preamble's guarantees would have very different meanings in the North and the South.

The Federalists lost control of the presidency in 1801, and the Congress that met in December of that year had a Republican majority in both houses. The Federalists had not entirely departed the scene, but their robust view of the national government and the Union had fewer and fewer advocates. One stood out: John Marshall of Virginia. Named Chief Justice of the High Court by outgoing President John Adams and confirmed by the Federalist majority in the lame duck Congressional session of 1801, Marshall's tenure on the Court from 1801 to 1835 ensured that the Federalists' view of the Preamble did not entirely disappear.

Marshall was born to the gentry in western Virginia in 1755 and inherited a plantation, but he preferred to live and work in Richmond. He saw combat as a young officer in the Revolution, served as a diplomat, and later as secretary of state (1800–1801). He never sought high elective office. Simple in dress, manner, and tastes, he rarely stood on ceremony and had little attachment to the aristocratic pretensions of the great Virginia Tidewater aristocracy. He was an admirable combination of doting husband, folksy town lawyer, entrepreneur and speculator (he had a huge law practice and invested in land schemes), deep thinker, principled believer in the prospects of the new nation, and political opportunist. In short, he embodied many of the contradictions and ironies of early national America.[1]

Marshall and Jefferson, though similar in background, came to detest one another. Marshall did not know that Jefferson was the author of the Kentucky Resolutions calling for nullification of the Alien and Sedition Acts (the notion that the state could nullify their imposition on its citizens), but the Chief Justice found them repellant. His view of the more perfect union was closer to Gouverneur Morris's. In *McCulloch v. Maryland* (1819), "a masterful opinion" written for a unanimous Court, Marshall explained why the Court

Chief Justice John Marshall, by Robert Matthew Sully.
*Courtesy of the Library of Congress, LC-DIG-det-4a31386.*

overturned a state tax on the congressionally chartered Second Bank of the United States in terms that Morris and Hamilton would have applauded. "The [federal] government proceeds directly from the people; it 'ordained and established' in the name of the people, and is declared to be ordained 'in order to form a more perfect union'.... The assent of the states, in their sovereign capacity, is implied, in calling a convention, and thus submitting that instrument to the people. But the people were at perfect liberty to accept or reject it; and their act was final. It required not the affirmance, and could not be negatived, by the state government. The constitution, when it was adopted, was of complete obligation, and bound the state sovereignties."[2]

Marshall read the Preamble back into the Constitution and no sooner was the opinion of the Court published than Marshall found himself under fire from supporters of states' rights, in particular some of the state supreme court justices. In reply, he wrote a series of newspaper editorials defending himself, though he published them anonymously. He insisted, "There is, then, no agreement formed between the government of the United States and those of the states. Our constitution is not a compact. It is the act of a single party. It is the act of the people of the United States, assembling in their respective states, and adopting a government for the whole nation." But Marshall's defense of his reading of federalism did not stop here. He continued, "Their motives for this act are assigned by themselves. They have specified the objects they intended to accomplish." To wit: they adopted a Preamble, and its clauses were clear indications of the purposes of the subsequent passages. In effect, he reversed Madison's notion that the Preamble's language and force was controlled by specific provisions of the rest of the Constitution. Marshall's Preamble was enforceable on its face. But Madison was not going to let Marshall have the last word.[3]

## Mr. Madison's Preamble

President Jefferson tried to drive the Federalist justices from the Court with impeachment, aiming ultimately at Marshall. Jefferson failed in this, but he won reelection in 1804 on a platform that rejected the Federalist views of the Preamble. The election of 1808 saw Jefferson's secretary of state and confidant, Madison, succeed him in the highest elective office. The Republicans controlled both houses, enabling Madison, who wanted to promote American trade abroad, to pursue a more aggressive policy toward Britain aimed at forcing open Britain's West Indian markets to American goods. Madison did not cite the common defense or the general welfare in support of this aggressive policy, however.

The election of 1810 put Madison under even more pressure to resist Britain's wartime policies, as the West and the South named a number of "war hawks" to Congress. These men included Henry Clay of Kentucky and John C. Calhoun of South Carolina. Clay was elected Speaker of the House of Representatives, a tribute to his ability to persuade others to accept his views, in this case that war was inevitable. On June 1, 1812, Madison asked Congress for a declaration of war. Outnumbered and beleaguered Federalists, who regarded the conflict as "Mr. Madison's War," dissented, but Congress passed a declaration by a decisive vote. Madison's message did not mention the common defense.

Madison did not want to give any credence to the Preamble. Nothing in the law as it stood then—no court decision, no jurisprudential commentary—said or implied that the Preamble was unenforceable. By not citing it, however, Madison came as close as he could to denying its potency. But if he was done with the Preamble, it was not done with his presidency. The debilities of prosecuting the War of 1812 convinced Calhoun and Clay that a better system of roads was necessary for national defense. In 1817, during his final days in office, Congress sent Madison a bill for federal sponsorship of a north–south road using the expected profits of funds in the deposit of the Second National Bank. On February 4, 1817, Calhoun had told the House of Representatives that the road was a legitimate federal project promoting general welfare and providing for the common defense. The former War Hawk wanted a national road system. The problem was one of defense over a great area. "In the recent war, how much did we suffer" for the want of good roads, Clay rhetorically asked. Clay also had defended the act under the General Welfare Clause of the Preamble. Even before the Constitution was written, Clay opined, a sense of the general welfare motivated the states to surrender their western lands to the confederation. Out of these grants the new state of Kentucky was formed. It was in the "welfare of our common country" that the "general government" paid for such improvements.[4]

Madison vetoed the Public Works Bill on March 3, 1817, just a day before he left office. Though the message was directed to Congress, Madison's real audience was Marshall and the ghost of Alexander Hamilton. "The legislative powers vested in Congress are specified and enumerated in the eighth section of the first article of the Constitution, and it does not appear that the power proposed to be exercised by the bill is among the enumerated powers, or that it falls by any just interpretation with the power to make laws necessary and proper for carrying into execution those or other powers vested by the Constitution in the Government of the United States." Marshall believed that the Preamble controlled the meaning of the Necessary and Proper Clause. Clay and Calhoun had relied on the General Welfare Clause of the Preamble to support the bill. Madison was not buying. "To refer the power in question to the clause 'to provide for common defense and general welfare' would be contrary to the established and consistent rules of interpretation, as rendering the special and careful enumeration of powers which follow the clause nugatory and improper. Such a view of the Constitution would have the effect of giving to Congress a general power of legislation instead of the defined and limited one hitherto understood to belong to them, the terms 'common defense and general welfare' embracing every object and act within the purview of a legislative trust." For Madison, were the federal government to undertake such projects, it would cross "the definite partition of powers between the General and the State Governments" on which "the permanent success of the Constitution depends."[5]

In retirement at his Montpelier estate, Madison responded to questions about his conduct in office, including his veto of the Bonus Bill. Behind these increasingly detailed and exasperated responses was a philosophy of government that quarantined the Preamble. It simply disappeared from his accounts of the drafting of the Constitution. He was on the committee that fashioned the Preamble. Presumably he could have given a dramatic or at least detailed narrative of its creation, but he did the exact opposite. He explained the meaning of the Preamble as if it had not come as the climax of the constitutional drafting process but as a kind of afterthought. For example, in a long and detailed 1830 letter to Andrew Stevenson, a Virginia congressman related to Madison's wife Dolley then serving as speaker of the House, describing how the general welfare and common defense came to be part of the Taxation Clause of Article I, he omitted any mention of how the same terms later appeared in the Preamble. It was as if the Preamble did not contain the two terms. Had he conceded this, he would have had to mention his collaboration with Morris and Hamilton on the Committee of Style. Instead, the letter became a vehicle to dispute the Federalist view of the Preamble.[6]

The letter, a brilliant piece of special pleading that deserves from students of the Constitution more attention than it has been given, has both a defensive and a pedantic tone, Madison lecturing the younger Stevenson. "In tracing the history and determining the import of the terms 'common defence and general welfare,' as found in the text of the Constitution, the following lights are furnished by the printed journal of the Convention which formed it." Madison also had at hand a copy of his own notes on the convention. "The terms appear in the general propositions offered May 29 [1787], as a basis for the incipient deliberations, the first of which 'Resolved, that the articles of the Confederation ought to be so corrected and enlarged as to accomplish the objects proposed by their institution, namely, common defence, security of liberty, and general welfare.'" By locating the two terms in the Articles, Madison associated them with limited government, his view of federalism, instead of with the Preamble. He argued that in the migration of the terms from the Articles to the Constitution they retained their initial, limited meaning—the revenue was to be raised and disbursed by Congress to pay the nation's bills, "as these general terms are prefixed in the like relation to the several legislative powers in the new charter as they were in the old, they must be understood to be under like limitations in the new as in the old." Madison, still sharp in his thinking, proposed that the introduction of "common defense and general welfare" into the Constitution from the Articles limited the powers of the future federal government. "With this addition, indeed, the language of the clause being in conformity with that of the clause in the Articles of Confederation, it would be qualified, as in those articles, by the specification of powers subjoined to it."

His account of the events at the convention is the most detailed historical tracing of what actually occurred, but Madison's history had less a scholarly than a political purpose. He wanted to separate the words in the Taxation Clause from the same words in the

Preamble. The Preamble was fashioned after the terms were added to the Taxation Clause, and according to commonly accepted constructions of law the Preamble should have controlled the interpretation of language written earlier. But the Preamble enlarged the terms, giving them broader application. (Or so Hamilton, along with Jay, Marshall, and Washington, concluded.) Hence Madison had to truncate the history, leaving out pieces of it—principally the drafting of the Preamble—to support his point. Madison's recounting of a sequence of reports, debates, and amendments in the convention all led, in Madison's view of the documentary record, to limit the power of Congress to the narrowest of fiscal activities. From his own notes, which were not published until after his death, as well as the official published proceedings ( he was careful to quote only the latter) he reported that on "September 4, the committee of eleven reported the following modification: 'The Legislature shall have power to lay and collect taxes, duties, imposts, and excises, to pay the debts and provide for the common defence and general welfare;' thus retaining the terms of the Article of Confederation, and covering, by the general term 'debts,' those of the old Congress. Thus introduced, however, they passed undisturbed through the subsequent stages of the Constitution."

Madison served on this committee with Gouverneur Morris, who could not have held this self-denying interpretation of the General Welfare Clause. A mere week later, with Madison's consent, Morris added the general welfare language to the Preamble, and there it had no limiting modifier. Madison did not mention any of this in the letter. Madison knew that Hamilton and the Federalists had not read the "general welfare" as limiting the collection and disbursement of revenue. They had seen the terms, in the light of the Preamble, as an invitation to expand the powers of Congress. If Madison could not explain away the construction Hamilton had given of the terms, he could, and did, simply ignore the Preamble.

With this sleight of hand, Madison was able to conclude that "The variations and vicissitudes in the modification of the clause in which the terms 'common defence and general welfare' appear, are remarkable, and to be no otherwise explained than by differences of opinion" rather than by differences in constitutional interpretation. Such differences of opinion underlay his veto message. "Consider for a moment the immeasurable difference between the Constitution limited in its powers to the enumerated objects, and expounded as it would be by the import claimed for the phraseology in question. The difference is equivalent to two Constitutions, of characters essentially contrasted with each other—the one possessing powers confined to certain specified cases, the other extended to all cases whatsoever."

This was the very language that Madison had employed in his veto message, here recast as the concluding passages in what purported to be an objective historical narrative of the framing of the Constitution. Madison prudently did not follow his history into the days when Hamilton and the nascent Federalist Party passed funding and assumption laws, or created a national bank over Madison's strenuous and fruitless opposition. Nor did he cite Jay in *Chisholm* nor Marshall in *McCulloch*. Instead, Madison closed with his own philosophy of government: "Allow me, my dear sir, to express on this occasion, what I always feel, an anxious hope that, as our Constitution rests on a middle ground between a form wholly national and one merely federal." Full recognition of the enforceability of the Preamble would have shifted that ground, and Madison did not want that to happen.

That philosophy faced an even sterner task in the Nullification Crisis of 1828–1833 when the issue shifted from general welfare and common defense to "a more perfect union." The Alien and Sedition Acts crisis passed when Jefferson was elected president and the Republicans gained majorities in both houses of Congress. But the words "compact" and "nullification" in his "Kentucky Resolves" were still available for anyone to use. A new generation of political thinkers and party leaders was free to draw conclusions of their own about the meaning of a more (or less) perfect union.

The "compact theory" of the Constitution and the doctrine of nullification would gain new life in 1828. Then, Calhoun relied upon the ideas in the Kentucky Resolves to justify South Carolina nullifying the Tariff Act of 1828. Calhoun was educated at Yale College and then prepared himself for a career as a lawyer at Tapping Reeve's school in Connecticut. Returning to South Carolina, he practiced off and on in his native state, but his major occupation was politics. He was an early advocate of universal male suffrage and when he entered national politics in 1810, he strongly supported a protective tariff, internal improvements, and expenditures for national defense,

John C. Calhoun, from a miniature by Blanchard, engraved by Archibald L. Dick, 1830.
*Courtesy of the Library of Congress, LC-USZ62-102297.*

including the national road project of 1816. What might have become a career of progressive reform nationalism sharply shifted as his prospects for the highest office dimmed. By the middle of the 1820s, his commitment to the nation had been replaced by an equally fervent sectionalism. The motive may have been a foreshortening of his ambition to be president, but his views closely paralleled those of other leading South Carolinians. Increasingly, they felt isolated from the major trends of national politics and economic development. The protective tariffs of the 1820s, culminating in the 1828 "tariff of abominations," favored the textile-producing states of the northeast over the cotton-exporting states of the southeast. In 1827, Calhoun wrote despairingly, "It seems to me, that the despotism founded on combined geographical interest [in Congress] admits of but one effectual remedy, a veto…on the part of the states."[7]

In his secretly authored "Exposition" for the South Carolina legislature's protest against the tariff, Calhoun proposed that the Constitution was not an organic and permanent form of government, but a contract or compact among sovereign states, and states could judge for themselves whether any act of the federal government applied to that state's citizens. It was a well-argued legal brief for nullification, the doctrine borrowed from the Kentucky Resolves and put to work to explain why the South Carolina legislature could pass a law preventing the collection of the tariff in South Carolina ports. South Carolina lawmakers would thereby decide for themselves the constitutionality of a federal law.

This flew in the face of the Constitution itself; Article I explicitly delegates to Congress the authority to lay tariffs, and Article VI states the Constitution and the laws made under it were the supreme law of the land. To support his contrary view of congressional power, Calhoun proposed that the Constitution was nothing more than a contract or compact among sovereign states, and over the course of many pages he developed this "compact theory." Under it, nullification was legitimate, though Calhoun, a lawyer, called for legal means to prevent the collection of the tariff. The majority of the newly elected South Carolina legislature threatened to use force if necessary—a foretaste of secession.[8]

Nullification was the very opposite of the more perfect Union that Madison and the framers promised. In an attempt to put the genie of nullification Jefferson had summoned up back in the bottle, Madison drafted a set of notes on nullification in late 1835. He denied that a state could nullify a federal law:

> A political system which does not contain an effective provision for a peaceable decision of all controversies arising within itself, would be a Govt. in name only. Such a provision is obviously essential; and it is equally obvious that it cannot be either peaceable or effective by making every part an authoritative umpire. The final appeal in such cases must be to the authority of the whole, not to that of the parts separately and independently. This was the view taken of the subject, whilst the Constitution was under the consideration of the people. It was this view of it which dictated the clause declaring that the Constitution & laws of the U. S. should be the supreme law of the Land, anything in the

const[itutio]n or laws of any of the States to the contrary not-withstanding.

For Madison, that was the only way that the nation could survive intact.[9]

In 1834, a weary Madison drafted a memo he entitled "Advice to My Country," a valedictory on the phrase "to form a more perfect union": "The advice nearest my heart and deepest in my convictions is that the Union of the States be cherished and perpetuated. Let the open enemy to it be regarded as a Pandora with her box opened; and the disguised one, as the serpent creeping with his deadly wiles into Paradise." Never a democrat (he always distrusted what true democracy would do to private property rights); never a believer in progressive government action (he always distrusted gatherings of the powerful); Madison's love of the Union was pure and unfailing.[10]

## Mr. Justice Story's Preamble

After the passing of the framers' generation, no one had more influence on the reading of the Preamble than Supreme Court Justice Joseph Story. He did not take part in writing the Constitution. He was a Republican by choice, but his views coincided with the Federalists' on many matters—but not the enforceability of the Preamble. His view of the Preamble was not part of a Supreme Court opinion and so was not "precedent." Indeed, his opinions were expressed away from the Court in a multi-volume set of classroom lectures he published in 1833. All this said, his views appeared in every serious discussion of the Preamble in his time and long after.

Born in 1779, Story came from a large Massachusetts family and found his way to Harvard and the law by diligent study. Indeed, he had a scholarly bent that he carried through his entire career. His frequent illnesses and the tragic deaths of his father and his wife drove him further into his books and his law practice. His second marriage was a happy one, though only two of his seven children survived to adulthood. A man of great personal honesty and conscience, he was an independent-minded Republican in state politics, and his brief term in Congress (December 1808–March 1809) saw him oppose Jefferson's foreign policy, an opposition that many New Englanders shared.

Justice Joseph Story.
*Courtesy of the Library of Congress, LC-DIG-cwpbh-02616.*

Story practiced law before the Court prior to his appointment to it in 1811. President Madison would not have named him to the Court, but his first two nominees failed to gain Senate approval and the third choice declined the nomination. Madison suspected Story's Republican credentials (a view that Jefferson shared in correspondence with Madison). Perhaps they were right—on the Court Chief Justice Marshall came to respect greatly Story's learning, and Story came to greatly admire the chief justice. Though they sometimes disagreed in detail (for example, Story favored stern government measures against the British during the War of 1812 while Marshall wanted to protect the American property of British nationals during the conflict), they shared a vision of a great nation bounded by law. Story more strongly opposed slavery than did Marshall, and Story found ways to free slaves when he could, a course that Marshall did not adopt.[11]

A born teacher, Story was named to a chair in law at Harvard Law School in 1829. His lectures became famous, and he turned them into much quoted commentaries on the law. These publications include treatises on equity, commercial law, and conflict of laws, subjects that connected private transactions to public law. He brought the same didactic style to the conferences of the Court, sometimes monopolizing the conversation. After Marshall died and the Court was dominated by Andrew Jackson's Democratic appointees, Story would carry the spirit of the Marshall Court into the new era. He died in 1845.[12]

As Dane professor of law at Harvard Law School, Story published his lectures in his various commentaries, the most respected, reprinted, and influential of which was his three-volume *Commentaries on the Constitution* (1833). Story revealed that his purpose in writing was not solely pedagogical. He thought that an authoritative exposition of the Constitution—authoritative not because he was an author (after all, Madison was still alive when Story wrote), but because the High Court had assumed unto itself the role of final arbiter of the meaning of the document. Story offered his views, "as may best enable the reader to estimate for himself the true value of each. In this way (as it is hoped) his judgment as well as his affections will be enlisted on the side of the Constitution, as the truest security of the Union, and the only solid basis, on which to rest the private rights, the public liberties, and the substantial prosperity of the people composing the American Republic."[13]

By 1833, the portion of the Preamble that seemed likely to clash with the "truest security of the Union" was the Blessings of Liberty Clause. Slavery was already the most divisive issue facing the Union. It had already caused sectional strife, and the rise of the abolitionist movement in the North was already causing Southerners to spout secessionist threats. The General Welfare Clause, insofar as it might enable Congress to pass laws inhibiting southern slave interest, could do as much damage to the Union as the Blessings of Liberty Clause. Both bottles had to be capped before their genies gained freedom.

As a justice, Story understood the challenge that slavery posed to the Union. That challenge changed his view of the Preamble. Writing for the Court in *Martin v. Hunter's Lessee* (1816), he explained: "The constitution of the United States was ordained and established, not by the states in their sovereign capacities, but emphatically, as the preamble of the constitution declares, by 'the people of the United States.' There can be no doubt that it was competent to the people to invest the general government with all the powers which they might deem proper and necessary; to extend or restrain these powers according to their own good pleasure, and to give them a paramount and supreme authority." As precedent (an opinion for the majority of the High Court sets precedent) Story's reading of the Preamble seemed to imply that it was fully enforceable. Marshall no doubt approved.[14]

But Story's 1833 comments on the Preamble in the *Commentaries* are uncharacteristically curt: "And, here, we must guard ourselves against an error, which is too often allowed to creep into the discussions upon this subject. The preamble never can be resorted to, to enlarge the powers confided to the general government, or any of its departments. It cannot confer any power per se; it can never amount, by implication, to an enlargement of any power expressly given. It can never be the legitimate source of any implied power, when otherwise withdrawn from the constitution. Its true office is to expound the nature, and extent, and application of the powers actually conferred by the constitution, and not substantively to create them." Story offered no legal precedent at all for this grand pronouncement. Indeed, if *Martin* and *McCulloch* were controlling, the precedent seemed to lie against Story's comment.[15]

But times had changed. No federal judge could now leave slavery out of his calculations. Story knew that slavery had brought Congress to its knees during the Missouri statehood crisis of 1819–1821, and members of Congress based their opposing views on their widely varying interpretations of the Constitution. That controversy literally went on just above where the Supreme Court sat in the old Senate chamber. He knew how vituperative the debates had become over the admission of Missouri as a slave state, and how close Henry Clay's compromise had come to failure. Both sides threatened disunion, but the loudest voices were southerners, and they seemed to speak as one. Attack slavery frontally and the South would secede.[16]

Story's *Commentaries* afforded slavery little space, and when he did, he made clear his personal dislike of the institution. Of the Fugitive Slave or Rendition Clause, the Constitution's most obvious concession to slavery, he wrote, "This clause was introduced into the constitution solely for the benefit of the slave-holding states, to enable them to reclaim their fugitive slaves, who should have escaped into other states, where slavery was not tolerated. The want of such a provision under the confederation was felt, as a grievous inconvenience, by the slave-holding states, since in many states no aid whatsoever would be allowed to the owners; and sometimes indeed they met with open resistance. In fact, it cannot escape the attention of every intelligent reader, that many sacrifices of opinion and feeling are to be found made by the Eastern and Middle states to the peculiar interests of the south. This forms no just subject of complaint; but it should for ever repress the delusive and mischievous notion, that the south has not at all times had its full share of benefits from the Union."[17]

And Story would not sacrifice the Union to his abhorrence of slavery. His decision meant that the Constitution must be made proof against the abolitionists. The one place where they might find comfort was the Blessings of Liberty Clause in the Preamble, but not if Story could deny it to them. "The constitution was, from its very origin, contemplated to be the frame of a national government, of special and enumerated powers, and not of general and unlimited powers." How did Story know this? Unlike Madison, he was not there, and had no hand in writing the Constitution. Madison's notes were not published until 1840, but Story had firsthand access over the years to other framers' accounts. "This is apparent, as will be presently seen, from the history of the proceedings of the convention, which framed it; and it has formed the admitted basis of all legislative and judicial reasoning upon it, ever since it was put into operation, by all, who have been its open friends and advocates, as well as by all, who have been its enemies and opponents."[18]

It was not clear who Story meant by "enemies and opponents." He did not explain. In general, he kept his passions closely guarded, and wrote generously of his own enemies and opponents. Typically, Story wrote of Madison to Ezekiel Bacon: "I entirely concur with you in your estimate of Mr. Madison—his private virtues, his extraordinary talents, his comprehensive and statesman-like views." The anti-federalists would have fit the category of enemies and opponents during the ratification period, but many of them had opted to serve in the new government, hardly the choice of unrelenting enemies and opponents. Story may have meant those who, like Calhoun, saw the Constitution as a compact among the states rather than a sovereign government itself. Story despised the compact theory and thought that Calhoun and those who followed him posed a threat to the very existence of the Union.[19]

Observing the nullification crisis swirling about him, Story concluded that any analysis of the Blessings of Liberty Clause in the Preamble based on the "intent" of the framers was fraught with problems. After all, Hamilton's intent and Morris's intent, particularly given their aversion to slavery, was to make the Preamble enforceable. One could mangle an account of the intent of particular framers, as Madison had and get away with it, for he had only to recall his own thoughts at the convention and after. Even he could not, however, know what was going on in Hamilton's mind, or King's, or Morris's, or Johnson's when they met and discussed Morris's draft. How much more difficult it would be for Story to probe these hidden recesses. Modern jurists who demand that courts interpret the Constitution in light of the particular aims of its framers have run into the same problem. Whether they rely on historical scholarship or view the primary sources themselves, such "originalists" can never know what was in the minds of the framers, even taking their surviving letters and other contemporary sources at face value.

Aware of all this long long before it became the subject of countless law review pieces in modern times, Story rejected naive interpretations of individual intent. He warned that "In the interpretation of a state statute, no man is insensible of the extreme danger of resorting to the opinions of those, who framed it, or those who passed it. Its terms may have differently impressed different minds. Some may have implied limitations and objects, which others would have rejected.…Some may have been governed by a temporary interest or excitement, and have acted upon that exposition, which most favoured their present views. Others may have seen lurking beneath its text, what commended it to their judgment against even present interests. Some may have interpreted its language strictly and closely; others from a different habit of thinking may have given it a large and liberal meaning." One could not ask for a better summary of the reasons for rejecting naive originalism.[20]

Story assayed a second kind of analysis of intent. He asked what was the meaning of the words to the entire Convention. This legal fiction of collective intent tracks the actions of the collective body of framers (in this case the Convention) as they drafted and revised the document. It reads intent by looking at changes to the parts of the document as they progress through their various stages. The Constitution created a sovereign national government. No theory, no doctrine, no special pleading could deny this. The Preamble was the surest guarantor of this position, but Story had already set aside the Preamble. He had declared it unenforceable to deny its "blessings of liberty" as the basis for a divisive attack on slavery. So Story had denied himself the most potent of all texts to serve his purpose. He had to scramble, leaving himself and the Constitution he so treasured open to the dragon's breath of disunion.

If the Constitution were considered to be an extension of the Articles of Confederation, then the Union was nothing more than a compact among the sovereign states and had no sovereignty apart from that conferred by the states. This was Calhoun's argument, and Story hurried to quash it. If Story had persuaded his reader that the Constitution did not confer unlimited powers on the federal government, he had still to hold off the other, equally pernicious doctrine that the general welfare could not have a national meaning. The compact theory would not go away, and Story knew it. Like Läocoon, the priest of Apollo at Troy attacked by two great snakes, Story had to hold both the consolidated government of Hamilton and the compact theory of Calhoun at a safe distance: "Stripped of the ingenious texture, by which this [compact theory] is disguised, it is neither more nor less, than an attempt to obliterate" the Union.[21]

In order to save the Constitution, its meaning must be fixed, and nowhere more so than in the effort to show that the Preamble was not directly enforceable, that the blessings of liberty were not meant for all Americans, and that the General Welfare Clauses enabled a national government to function while not intruding over much in state sovereignty. A loose cannon, the Preamble's language must be tied down with the heavy tackle of constitutional theory. As Story wrote in the *Commentaries*, the Constitution "is to have a fixed, uniform, permanent construction," and that "so far...as human infirmity will allow," it "should be...the same yesterday, today, and for ever."[22]

Story had donned the mantle of the framers. He was entitled to wear it. No one of his generation (and few who followed him) have thought as hard and written as precisely about the meaning of the Constitution as he. But his great fear—the dissolution of the Union—could not be averted by even as prudently parsed readings of the Preamble. He did not live to hear abolitionist Wendell Phillips say "that the lesson of the hour is insurrection" in a salute to John Brown after his raid on Harper's Ferry, or, in the weeks after secession, demand that the North seceded from the South because "our ship of state is going to pieces on the lee shore of slavery." He did not live to hear Alexander Stephens warn the Georgia Secession Convention, "This step of secession, once taken, can never be recalled. And all the withering and baleful consequences that must follow, will rest on this convention. When we and our posterity shall see our lovely South desolated by the demon of war, which this act of yours will inevitably invite and call forth…who but this convention will be held responsible for it?" He did not live to hear these words, but Story saw it coming, sectional disputes leading to nullification and nullification breeding secession. Secession and Civil War, horrible as they were for him to contemplate, would become the great tests for the Preamble. In those tests, the preamble's promises were remolded and set at the head of a very different kind of government—a government in which liberty and justice for all, in the words of Abraham Lincoln, would begin to be more than an empty promise.[23]

## Abraham Lincoln's Preamble

Joseph Story deeply believed that the Constitution was written for all generations and the Union was perpetual. Indeed, "We the People…do ordain and establish…for ourselves" was a hallmark of the founding generation, claiming the great work of constitution-making as their own. Would that Union endure its greatest challenge—the challenge of secession?

After the election of Republican presidential candidate Abraham Lincoln in 1860, the South Carolina legislature called for a special convention to decide whether the state would depart the federal Union. The delegates agreed that the victorious Republicans in Washington, D.C., posed a grave threat to the future of slavery. By excluding slavery from the western territories, limiting the internal slave trade, and otherwise hindering the legal rights of slave owners, Republican majorities in Congress and a Republican president might undermine the very foundations of the state's wealth and its social system. The unanimous decision of that convention to secede posed a devastating threat to the Union's survival.[24]

The framers of the South Carolina convention's Declaration adopted John C. Calhoun's interpretation of the Constitution as a compact among sovereign states. "We hold that the Government thus established [under the federal Constitution] is subject to…a…fundamental principle, namely: the law of compact. We maintain that in every compact between two or more parties, the obligation is mutual; that the failure of one of the contracting parties to perform a material part of the agreement, entirely releases the obligation of the other." In so doing, they rejected key portions of the language of the Preamble. "We the People of the United States" became "we the states." "A more perfect union" gave way to a permanently imperfect union, subject to states exercising their right to depart. "Domestic tranquility" turned into domestic disorder, beginning with the violent silencing of Unionists in the state. In a society where slavery would be even more entrenched than in the United States as a whole, the scope of the "blessings of liberty" shrank to those blessing a certain status, race, and gender could claim. The "common defense" meant defending secession against all its critics, and the general welfare corresponded to the welfare of the slave owner.[25]

With that resolution, South Carolina regarded itself as having departed the Union. It was soon joined by Georgia, Alabama, Mississippi, Louisiana, Florida, and Texas. Calhoun's compact theory of the Constitution was the grounds relied upon, ironically, to defend the very event that Calhoun most feared—the dismemberment of the United States. But the irony did not end there. When delegates to a March 1861 convention in Montgomery, Alabama, drafted a constitution for the Confederate States of America, they prefaced it, "We, the people of the Confederate States, each State acting in its sovereign and independent character, in order to form a permanent federal government, establish justice, insure domestic tranquillity, and secure the blessings of liberty to ourselves and our posterity." The framers borrowed selectively from the Preamble. The document, largely the work of Georgia jurist and legal scholar Thomas R. R. Cobb, implied that the new confederacy was to be permanent, a contradiction in terms if the right of secession was the very essence of the "sovereign and independent character" of each state. Legal contradictions to one side, by the end of April, Virginia, North Carolina, Tennessee, and Arkansas would join the breakaway states. All eleven ratified the new constitution, though as events would prove, it would have a short life span.[26]

The "our posterity" in the preface to the Confederate constitution had a different connotation than the same phrase in the federal Constitution. The framers of 1787 assumed that "our posterity" was all the citizens of the United States to come. Our posterity—in their minds—was not divisible, partible, or otherwise subject to diminution. It was an expansive phrase, fitting an "empire of freeholders, spreading endlessly into the West, making an old land forever new." It was a phrase growing out of a revolution in which elites had to listen to those new to power, to "ordinary people."[27]

"Our posterity" in the context of the Montgomery document's preamble implied something entirely different. Although Cobb may have simply been looking for a glowing phrase to suggest the longevity of the new government, that was not the way he used words. His magnum opus, a heavily documented, thoroughly researched treatise on the law of slavery showed him to be a scholar, not a penman. It took him nearly a decade to research and write. Deeply conservative, sincerely religious, he believed that all government was founded on natural laws. These governed the social relations of men and women, and of the races. As he wrote in that treatise on the law of slavery published three years before he joined his fellow secessionists in Montgomery, some institutions (in particular slavery) were "more universal than marriage, and more permanent than liberty." In this sense, "our posterity" was not a people defined politically, but a people defined by enduring cultural ways. Our posterity was something akin to our set, our class, our sort of people, or, most simply, us. Such an inclusive definition fit the Confederacy.[28]

So long as the outcome of the war was in doubt, secession posed a mortal danger to the federal Constitution and the Union for which it stood. The purposes for which the Union was founded were expressed in the Preamble. Not surprisingly, then, the Civil War Era focused the attention of Unionists on its language. The rethinking of the Preamble did not spring at once from the frantic efforts of Lincoln's cabinet and the Republican Party in Congress to save the Union. Deeds, not words, saved the Union. But over the course of four years of heroic and horrific deeds, followed by the Reconstruction Era (1865–1877), the clauses of the Preamble gained new solidity and force.

The opening rounds of the Civil War began the process. Outgoing President James Buchanan had told Congress that the Union was indissoluble, "The preamble to the Constitution of the United States, having express reference to the Articles of Confederation, recites that it was established 'in order to form a more perfect union.' And yet it is contended that this 'more perfect union' does not include the essential attribute of perpetuity. But that the Union was designed to be perpetual appears conclusively from the nature and extent of the powers conferred by the Constitution on the Federal Government. These powers embrace the very highest attributes of national sovereignty." But for Buchanan the United States was still a union of states, and the crisis could only be resolved by the seceding states agreeing to return to the Union. His hands, he thought, were tied.[29]

President Abraham Lincoln read the Preamble's "We the People" differently. On July 4, 1861, Lincoln sent a message to a special session of the Congress he had convened. He was a Union man, of that there was no doubt. As he scribbled to himself two months before his inauguration, "Without the Constitution and the Union, we could not have attained the result; but even these, are not the primary cause of our great prosperity. There is something back of these, entwining itself more closely about the human heart. That something, is the principle of 'Liberty to all' the principle that clears the path for all gives hope to all and, by consequence, enterprize, and industry to all." In the four months since his inauguration, facing the intransigence of the seceding states, Lincoln had begun the task of turning a slow moving, deliberative, small and weak national government into an energetic leviathan, enlisting and arming men, seeking funding, and beginning the process of staffing a huge bureaucracy. Where was the constitutional sanction for this? Lincoln saw it in the Constitution itself. While others of less conviction might wring their hands at the inevitable dissolution of the Union, he had no doubt that the Constitution provided the means for its own defense.[30]

The specific purpose of Lincoln's message was to reassure and to explain, not to apologize, for his vigorous suppression of anti-Union activities. He had already authorized military arrests of civilians and denied habeas corpus relief to the arrestees. Necessity dictated his conduct. "It might seem, at first thought, to be of little difference

Abraham Lincoln: President-elect, by Samuel G. Alschuler.
*Courtesy of the Library of Congress, LC-USZ62-15984.*

whether the present movement at the South be called 'secession' or 'rebellion.' The movers, however, well understand the difference." Words, to Lincoln at least, still mattered. A courtroom master of cross-examination and final summation, words were his tools. "At the beginning, they knew they could never raise their treason to any respectable magnitude, by any name which implies violation of law. They knew their people possessed as much of moral sense, as much of devotion to law and order, and as much pride in, and reverence for, the history, and government, of their common country, as any other civilized, and patriotic people"[31]

The Constitution defined treason as levying war against the United States. The secessionists claimed that they no longer were citizens of the United States. Lincoln never accepted that claim.

A more perfect Union could not countenance secession. His own Union sentiment was so strong that Lincoln assumed it must reach deeply into southern hearts. He presumed that the secessionists "knew they could make no advancement directly in the teeth of these strong and noble sentiments. Accordingly they commenced by an insidious debauching of the public mind." Lincoln was not entirely right. Although there was great Unionist sentiment in the South, secession was by no means unpopular among southern white men. While some Unionists were cowed into silence or became convinced that they must hold their tongues, Lincoln probably exaggerated the extent of Unionism, particularly after secession was complete.[32]

Then whom exactly did Lincoln have in mind when he accused the secessionists of an insidious debauching of the public mind? John C. Calhoun's compact theory was the centerpiece of the constitutional defense of secession, but Calhoun was over a decade in his grave. Lincoln's real target was Mississippi's Jefferson Davis, a former U.S. Senator and secretary of war, now the president of the Confederacy. Davis's inaugural address in April 1861 rested the case for secession on Calhoun's compact theory. Lincoln sneered at it: "The sophism itself is, that any state of the Union may, consistently with the national Constitution, and therefore lawfully, and peacefully, withdraw from the Union, without the consent of the Union, or of any other state. The little disguise that the supposed right is to be exercised only for just cause, themselves to be the sole judge of its justice, is too thin to merit any notice."[33]

But contumely did not strengthen the sinews of a nation gearing up for Civil War. Instead, Lincoln offered meatier fare: an analysis of the meaning of a more perfect union comparable to anything Madison attempted, but entirely different in its use of the Preamble. "This [compact theory] derives much—perhaps the whole—of its currency, from the assumption, that there is some omnipotent, and sacred supremacy, pertaining to…each State of our Federal Union." But the nature of state sovereignty changed fundamentally when they agreed to become part of the Union. The Constitution limned out that changed status. "Our States have neither more, nor less power, than that reserved to them, in the Union, by the Constitution—no one of them ever having been a State out of the Union." The states of the United States in 1788 were not the same as the states before the Constitution went into effect! New states were only states because they were accepted into the Union. Their sovereignty depended upon the Constitutional provisions for admission to the Union, not upon some preternatural statehood. Of the confederate states, Alabama, Mississippi, Arkansas, Florida, Louisiana, and Texas only were states because they were accepted into the Union. "The new ones…only took the designation of States, on coming into the Union.…Having never been States, either in substance, or in name, outside of the Union, whence this magical omnipotence of 'State rights,' asserting a claim of power to lawfully destroy the Union itself?" This, then, was how a more perfect Union formed: The states' independent existence dissolved when they ratified the Constitution and were reborn after they ratified; the Union incorporating new lands as states equal to those already joined. "The States have their status IN the Union, and they have no other legal status. If they break from this, they can only do so against law, and by revolution."

Lincoln was not arguing for the consolidation of government along Hamiltonian lines, nor for the abrogation of state governments. Northern states claimed for themselves a degree of sovereignty, and Lincoln needed northern state support to win the Civil War. But that sovereignty was conferred on them by the Constitution. "Unquestionably the States have the powers, and rights, reserved to them in, and by the National Constitution." Again, the states' sovereignty derived from their place in the Union.

At bottom, that Union was a gathering of all the people, not just the people of some of the states. The Preamble said it all: "These [secessionist] politicians are subtle, and profound, on the rights of minorities. They are not partial to that power which made the Constitution, and speaks from the preamble, calling itself 'We, the People.'" For the bedrock of Lincoln's constitutional case was the argument that the Union rested upon the people's will, in effect that a more perfect Union was a union that incorporated more and more of "We the People." Secession was the opposite of this, because it left out more and more of the people. "It may well be questioned whether there is, to-day, a majority of the legally qualified voters of any State, except perhaps South Carolina, in favor of disunion. There is much reason to believe that the Union men are the majority in many, if not in every other one, of the so-called seceded States."

Whether Lincoln was right or wrong in fact (a fact almost impossible to prove or disprove, for the strength of Unionist sentiment might vary), his assertion tied the More Perfect Union Clause to "We the People" with dissoluble bonds. "It may be affirmed, without extravagance, that the free institutions we enjoy, have developed the powers, and improved the condition, of our whole people, beyond any example in the world." It was only possible within the Union, and the dissolution of the Union would devolve the processes of greater democracy. The nation would backslide into dissension and disorder. The Confederacy would soon lose the characteristics of a constitutional democracy and mutate into a government of the few over the many.[34]

Lincoln closed with a kind of sadness, for it was necessity, not his own desire, that he had to use force. The Constitution imposed this duty on him, and he did not suppose that the Union was made more perfect by the deployment of a great army to compel his fellow countrymen in the South to obey the law. "It was with the deepest regret that the Executive found the duty of employing the war-power, in defence of the government, forced upon him. He could but perform this duty, or surrender the existence of the government." The common defense was the defense of the people against a handful of conniving and sinister secessionists. The people had spoken in the election of 1860. He was their servant. "He felt that he had no moral right to shrink; nor even to count the chances of his own life, in what might follow," a tragic prophecy fulfilled by an assassin's bullet.

.................

The Union, and with it the Preamble to the Constitution, survived secession and war. Despite Madison's refusal to credit its potential and Story's dictum that it was unenforceable, Lincoln found in the Preamble a formidable source of authority for the defense of union, democracy, and human rights. In the years following the war, American jurists and lawmakers should have turned to the Preamble for guidance in reconstructing the union. For a brief time, that is exactly what happened.

# CHAPTER 6

## Legacies of the Preamble

The Civil War required a vast expansion of the federal government in personnel, expenditure, and, finally, in constitutional law itself. For Southern rebellion in the names of states' rights led, in an ironic sequence of events, to a fundamental reconceptualization of federalism in the North. Three so-called Reconstruction Amendments profoundly changed the relationship between the federal government and the states. The thirteenth ended slavery; the fourteenth defined citizenship as national rather than state, and required the states to guarantee due process, equal protection of the law, and the privileges or immunities of all citizens to those residing in the state; and a fifteenth barred states from denying the right to vote on the basis of race. For a time—but only for a time—it seemed as though Madison's and Story's ideal of a limited federalism had fallen, releasing the Preamble from the restraints in which they had confined it.

## The Preamble in Reconstruction

The Reconstruction Amendments enforced the promise of the Preamble. The last clause of each of the three empowered Congress to pass legislation to further their aims. A congressional majority framed civil rights laws to insure that the freedmen and women enjoyed the blessings of liberty and established justice. As Charles Sumner, one of the leaders of that majority in the Senate, told an audience at the Cooper Institute in New York City two years after the war ended, the Preamble's invocation of "We the People" was inseparable from "a constant dedication to human rights." At last, millions of Americans whose skin color and condition of servitude had excluded them from "We the People" were incorporated in the body politic.[1]

The road to the Reconstruction Amendments was not smoothly paved. In September 1862, Lincoln warned those states still in rebellion that their slave property would be forfeit as contraband. On January 1, 1863, the Emancipation Proclamation kept that promise. Henceforth, those slaves were free—though they would have to brave all the dangers of finding the Union lines to enjoy that freedom. But the emancipation of the slaves did not rest solely upon Lincoln's inherent powers as commander in chief. It was the completion of that part of the Preamble foreseen by Rufus King, Gouverneur Morris, and their abolitionist descendants. The Thirteenth Amendment was a gloss on the Blessings of Liberty Clause in the Preamble. Nothing had changed in the constitutional universe except slavery. Maybe this was enough. "Even the abolitionist movement could not decide whether the Amendment was an end or a beginning." But perhaps the question did not matter. For the Amendment meant that the blessings of liberty at last included all Americans.[2]

After the War, black abolitionists, deriving some of their argument from their white comrades, had the best answer to all of these circumlocutions. The Constitution's preamble began "We the People," not "We Some of the People"; nor "We the People Who Own Property"; nor even "We the White People." Even if slaves had been considered solely as property under Southern states' laws, free people of color were not property. If they were debarred from voting or holding office or sitting on juries or testifying under oath in the free states, they were still people under the federal Constitution. Nowhere in the Constitution was white or black ever mentioned, until slavery was ended. No color was ever required or barred in the election of members of congress, judges, or members of the executive branch. A year after the Civil War was over, Virginia's black congressman John Mercer Langston explained: "In no article or paragraph of our Constitution did Washington and his noble compeers, either in direct terms or logical inferences, by any complexional discrimination, deny to any class of our people their rights and privileges. The Constitution is rather the strong palladium of our freedom—guarding, protecting, and defending all those rights which pertain to an American citizen." Taney was two years in his grave when Langston added a belated tenth justice's reading of *Dred Scott*.[3]

Freed of the shackles that Madison and Story fastened to it, elevated by the Reconstruction Amendments and the Civil Rights Acts, the Preamble might have taken its rightful place among the landmarks of American constitutionalism. But that event was not to be. For just as the great experiment in Reconstruction was empowering the language of the Preamble, so resistance to that experiment by so-called Southern Redeemers (formerly Democrats, later Confederates, who wanted to control Southern politics as they had before the war) once more confined the Preamble's promises to empty rhetoric.

To reenter the Union under the plan that Lincoln had outlined and President Andrew Johnson implemented after Lincoln's death, ten percent of the white male population of each of the former confederate states had to sign loyalty oaths and the state had to ratify the Thirteenth Amendment. With the hostilities ended, the newly conquered South did not accept the full implications of the Amendment its states ratified. Domestic tranquility in the Reconstruction Era was anything but insured, nor was justice established in the conquered South. Returning confederate veterans, including their officers, were averse to their former slaves gaining title to the land (a plan favored by some radical Republicans), much less treating former slaves as equals. Freedmen and women were harassed, belittled, and cheated by their white neighbors as whites tried to "redeem" the South from the influence of the Republicans and their black allies. Newly reconstructed state governments no sooner ratified the Thirteenth Amendment and fulfilled the other terms required for their readmission to the Union than their legislatures passed vagrancy laws effectively re-enslaving the blacks. Mississippi's provisions were typical of the 1865 "black codes": "Every civil officer shall, and every person may, arrest and carry back to his or her legal employer any freedman, free negro, or mulatto who shall have quit the service of his or her employer before the expiration of his or her term of service without good cause."[4]

The Republican majority in Congress watched in mounting concern as these black codes were enforced by state authorities aided by terrorist groups like the Ku Klux Klan. The testimony of former slaves at Congressional hearings documented the outrages.

No one could miss the mounting evidence of white-on-black vio-lence. Congress passed civil rights acts, but the laws did not enforce themselves, and mounting violence in the South made a mockery of federal law.[5]

A recognition of that failure was the Supreme Court's decision in *United States v. Cruikshank* (1875). In the wake of a contested 1872 election year in Louisiana, a white militia armed with rifles and a small cannon overpowered and assassinated a group of former slaves at the parish courthouse in Colfax, Louisiana. Most of the freedmen were killed after they surrendered, and nearly fifty were killed later that night after being held as prisoners for several hours. The U.S. attorney for the state ordered the arrest of the ringleaders of the massacre and brought them to trial for violating the freed-men's civil rights. After three trials in New Orleans, three of the defendants were convicted, but Supreme Court Justice Joseph Brad-ley, sitting on the bench at the trial, ruled that the act under which they were indicted was unconstitutional and ordered all the men set free.[6]

When the federal prosecutors appealed the case, it was heard by the full U.S. Supreme Court. Chief Justice Morrison R. Waite wrote for all but one of his colleagues. He found all of the six-teen indictments under the civil rights act void for vagueness and other technical errors. More important, perhaps, was the way that Waite read the Fourteenth Amendment to detach it from the Pre-amble. Framed to empower Congress to pass enforcement acts, to the Court's majority the Amendment seemed to impose limitations on Congress, much as Madison read the Taxation Clause to impose limitations on what Congress could do under the General Welfare Clause. The act under which the perpetrators were tried was faulty, because it could only apply to individuals when they were agents or officers of the state, not when they acted in their private capac-ity. In short, the enforcement act under which the prosecutions were brought was itself unconstitutional, because the Fourteenth Amendment, under which the Enforcement Act was passed, said "no state shall...." The Court invented this "state action" doctrine, and it limited what federal prosecutors could do in civil rights cases. The Preamble's invocation of "domestic tranquility" had vanished, along with the commitment to establish justice and the promise of the blessings of liberty.

Punishment for the murder of the freedmen was left to the state of Louisiana's courts, the High Court knowing that no such prosecutions would be brought, and none were. As Waite intoned, "We have in our political system a government of the United States and a government of each of the several States. Each one of these governments is distinct from the others, and each has citizens of its own who owe it allegiance, and whose rights, within its jurisdiction, it must protect." A robust concept of states' rights after the war had done what the secession movement could not do—protect the absolute authority of an armed white population to brutalize its black fellow citizens. Even though the blacks were also citizens of the United States, "The duty of a [federal] government to afford protection is limited always by the power it possesses for that purpose." In a less than admirable irony, Waite had quoted the Preamble against itself.

The long history of Jim Crow segregation, of lynching, and of almost casual white-on-black violence proceeded apace from so-called Redemption of the South well into the twentieth century. While the federal courts may have been (or declared themselves to be) powerless to prevent such outrages, the retreat from the ideals of the Preamble gave a patina of legality to the Jim Crow regime.[7]

Not everyone accepted this outcome. In vain had the lone dissenter in *Plessy v. Ferguson* (1896), the case finding that Louisiana's separate rail car law was constitutional, Justice John Marshall Harlan, read the Thirteenth and Fourteenth Amendments in light of the Preamble: "The Thirteenth Amendment does not permit the withholding or the deprivation of any right necessarily inhering in freedom. It not only struck down the institution of slavery as previously existing in the United States, but it prevents the imposition of any burdens or disabilities that constitute badges of slavery or servitude. It decreed universal civil freedom in this country. This court has so adjudged. But that amendment having been found inadequate to the protection of the rights of those who had been in slavery, it was followed by the Fourteenth Amendment, which added greatly to the dignity and glory of American citizenship, and to the security of personal liberty." But Harlan could not hold out against the tide. As he conceded, writing for a unanimous U.S. Supreme Court in 1906, "Although that Preamble indicates the general purposes for which the people ordained and established the Constitution, it has never been regarded as the source of any substantive power conferred on the Government of the United States or on any of its Departments." That was not historically true, as we have seen, but now, with the imprimatur of the High Court, Story's out-of-doors dictum became constitutional orthodoxy.[8]

For modern Americans, Jim Crow, the popular term for the system of formal and informal segregation imposed on black people in the South, seems the very antithesis of the "blessings of liberty" promised in the Preamble and the casual violence of lynching the very opposite of domestic tranquility, but for those who imposed the system and those who later supported it, the injunctions of the Preamble had no weight. From Presidents like Woodrow Wilson, to Justices of the U.S. Supreme Court like Henry Billings Brown (who wrote *Plessy*), down to the local sheriffs and judges who looked the other way when mobs and vigilantes enforced Jim Crow, the liberty to oppress was the only liberty that mattered.[9]

## The Preamble in the New Deal

The Preamble was a threatening text for those who wanted to limit the intrusion of the federal government into everyday life, particularly when that intrusion imposed unwanted civic duties on private individuals. Thus the retreat from Reconstruction reforms had to deny the Preamble any authority as law. But when people turned to the federal government to help the needy and relieve the oppressed, the Preamble once more became a source of constitutional succor. After the nation stumbled into what seemed to be an endless economic crisis after the stock market crash of 1929 and the massive unemployment that followed, the Preamble's language of government responsibility for the general welfare once more moved to center stage.

The "New Deal" from 1933 to 1941 featured two sets of legislative initiatives. In the first, from Franklin Delano Roosevelt's election to mid-1935, the president, with the compliance of Congress, experimented with fiscal and relief programs. These lacked a clear ideological and structural base, and included cost-cutting measures, devaluation of the currency, direct grants to cities and states, and federal works projects. Larger programs ranged from the Agricultural Adjustment Act, with price setting, production quotas, and payments for reduced planting, to the National Industrial Recovery Act and its National Recovery Administration which managed the manufacturing side of the economy. The U.S. Supreme Court struck down many of these enactments. With the Depression largely unaffected by the first New Deal, in 1935 the Roosevelt administration considered more basic egalitarian reforms. Among these were programs to provide jobs (the Works Progress Administration), the Social Security Act, the Rural Electrification Administration, and the National Labor Relations Act. Again opponents of the legislation would turn to the High Court. Over the course of three years, from 1935 to 1938, lawyers for the federal government, lawyers for private industry, and the justices themselves would revisit Hamilton's, Madison's, and Story's views on the Preamble in the effort to defend, overturn, and adjudicate the Second New Deal.[10]

When Secretary of Agriculture Henry Wallace and Attorney General Homer Cummings gave widely covered speeches defending the Congress's general welfare powers, conservatives wrote angry letters to the *New York Times* and the *Washington Post* attacking the speeches and their underlying rationale of a broadly construed General Welfare Clause by invoking Madison's writings. Liberals rejoined by citing Hamilton's views, an ironic reversal of the economic positions that Madison and Hamilton held in the 1790s. On April 12, 1933, Alexander Sidney Lanier, a conservative military lawyer, blasted the New Deal. "In fact, it seems futile these days to raise constitutional questions…it would appear that the Constitution has become only an instrument of academic and antiquarian interest." Lanier was ahead of the curve, but the pack soon followed. The *Times* editorialized that "many things have been done under the New Deal for which it is hard to find specific constitutional warrant. If only everything could be justified by the general welfare clause it would make the work of legislation much easier. The reference is, of course, to the Preamble of the Constitution." Imagine if the other clauses of the Preamble were given such weight, the *Times* smirked; "why not seek a judicial interpretation of the purpose to 'insure domestic tranquility,' for example. Should not Congress propose uniform marriage laws?" But the tongue-in-cheek editorial was not intended as a lesson in history. "If the preamble could be made a fountain from which to draw water for every thirsty soul, this clause could be invoked against every restriction upon the citizen."[11]

Harvard Law School–trained attorney and author Samuel Boyd Darling was not amused by the editorial, and he thought Hamilton would not be amused either. According to Darling's letter to the editor, the *Times* editorial writer had missed the second general welfare clause "elsewhere in the Constitution." That clause, according to Hamilton and Darling, did give to Congress a broad legislative mandate. John Jansen agreed with Darling that the Congress had relied not on the Preamble but on the Taxation Clause. But other contributors to the *Times* came to the defense of its editorial. Alfred Lilienthal and David Du Vivier opined that "legally, this position would be indefensible." Lilienthal, a first-year law student at Columbia University at the time and former member of the Young Republicans club, cited as authority none other than Joseph Story, on whose reluctance to find any such general welfare powers the Court had relied on "time and again." Lilienthal argued that Hamilton had tried "six times" to gain acceptance for "broad congressional power to legislate for any and every object that might benefit the people" and failed. In fact, Hamilton's domestic program had never been reviewed by the High Court, and had it been, it would probably have been found constitutional (the Court consisting of Jay, Wilson, and other strong Federalists at the time).[12]

By 1935, the dispute over the Preamble arrived at the High Court. In *Schechter v. U.S.* (1935), commonly referred to as the "sick chicken case," the General Welfare Clauses figured prominently in the Court's opinion. The Court unanimously struck down the National Industrial Recovery Act of 1933 and the National Recovery Administration, both premised on the General Welfare Clause. Counsel for the New York City poultry company dismissed any claim "upon a non-existent power in the Federal Government to enact any act deemed by it necessary or desirable to promote the general welfare," apparently a winning argument against a Federalist reading of the Preamble.[13]

In *United States v. Butler* (1936), striking down the cotton production provisions of the Agricultural Adjustment Act of 1933, the Supreme Court denied that Congress could legislate for the general welfare in any manner it chose. The General Welfare Clause inched closer to the front and center of the Court's purview because the government hoped to find a new foundation on which to base its case, and showcased the Preamble. Henry A. Wallace led the charge.

Speaking to the Connecticut Council of Churches, he pleaded that "building up a stronger sense of the general welfare" was the only way to stop the insidious corruption of government by "pressure groups." Attorney General Cummings was more precise, promising that "these expectations of general welfare" would bring benefits "to the entire nation."[14]

With the shift to a full debate in oral argument over the clauses, Madison, Hamilton, and Story stepped to the front of the briefs, oral argument, and opinions. Solicitor General Stanley Forman Reed put the government's case before the Court in *Butler* firmly on general welfare grounds—the Depression was a national emergency affecting the general welfare, and Congress had acted accordingly. "We contend that the general welfare clause gave Congress power to expend it for rental and benefit payments....The general welfare clause should be construed broadly to include anything conducive to the national welfare; it is not limited by the subsequently enumerated powers....That this, commonly known as the Hamiltonian theory, is correct, is shown by the plain language of the clause; by the circumstances surrounding its adoption; by the opinion of most of those who participated in the early execution of the Constitution; by the opinion of later authorities; and by long-continued practical construction."[15]

Counsel for the cotton industry, Pennsylvania's George Wharton Pepper, a legal scholar as well as a litigator, replied in kind, regarding the debate between Hamilton and Madison over the first Bank of the United States in a different light. "I understand Madison's view to have been that the [general] welfare for which Congress may appropriate is the welfare which may be achieved in the exercise of the granted powers. I understand the Hamiltonian view to have been that, irrespective of the existence of power in virtue of specific grants or implications, the power to tax may be used to raise revenue for the general welfare, and that appropriations may be made out of that fund for such purposes as Congress may think fit. But I did not know, until this statute proposed it, of any interpretation which begins where Hamilton stops, and asserts that because you may appropriate for anything which congress thinks is consonant with the public welfare, you may, through that appropriation, control the local conduct of the producer in a particular reserved to the States under the Tenth Amendment. That, it seems to me, is the general welfare clause gone mad."[16]

Reed replied with more historical evidence. "The scope of the welfare clause has never been finally decided by this Court. The Government's position is not that it may take any action it pleases under the welfare clause.... This interpretation of the welfare clause has met the approval of those who participated in the ratifying conventions. It met the approval of George Washington when he sent his message to Congress that agriculture should be supported and benefitted by Congressional appropriations.... That is the interpretation of the welfare clause which has met the approval of commentators from Story to Justice Miller."[17]

Justice Owen Roberts, who wrote the majority opinion for himself and four other members of the Court, seemed to view the government's case with skepticism. In particular, he offered his own reading of Story's *Commentaries*. "The view that the clause grants power to provide for the general welfare, independently of the taxing power, has never been authoritatively accepted. Mr. Justice Story points out that if it were adopted 'it is obvious that under color of the generality of the words, to "provide for the common defence and general welfare," the government of the United States is, in reality, a government of general and unlimited powers, notwithstanding the subsequent enumeration of specific powers.'"[18]

At the same time, Roberts weighed the historical evidence in a way that seemed to favor the New Deal advocates' stance. "Since the foundation of the Nation sharp differences of opinion have persisted as to the true interpretation of the phrase....Hamilton...maintained the clause confers a power separate and distinct from those later enumerated, is not restricted in meaning by the grant of them, and Congress consequently has a substantive power to tax and to appropriate, limited only by the requirement that it shall be exercised to provide for the general welfare of the United States....Each contention has had the support of those whose views are entitled to weight." Roberts' history was a little flawed, however. He misread Story: "Mr. Justice Story, in his Commentaries, espouses the Hamiltonian position."[19]

Hamilton would have been pleased by this conclusion, and Madison would have been bewildered, for Story took a middle path. This questionable reading of the history of the clauses to one side, Roberts continued: "We shall not review the writings of public men and commentators or discuss the legislative practice. Study of all these leads us to conclude that the reading advocated by Mr. Justice Story is the correct one." Story was not a framer; he was, like Roberts, a Supreme Court justice. But his opinions on the Preamble were not expressed from the bench, and thus were not precedent. Harlan's opinion was given in an opinion for the Supreme Court, and so was precedent, but Harlan's source was not case law. It was Story's treatise. All in all, Roberts' was a rather striking misreading of Story, and it had an even more striking impact on the law, for Roberts wrote as if Story's words were precedent. "It results that the power of Congress to authorize expenditure of public moneys for public purposes is not limited by the direct grants of legislative power found in the Constitution." In other words, the General Welfare Clause gave Congress power to tax and spend for matters not specifically enumerated in Article I. In so doing, the Court omened that it would not limit the power to tax and spend.[20]

Justice Roberts has never been placed in the pantheon of great jurists. A Philadelphia lawyer and Republican moderate, he was President Herbert Hoover's nominee and had no trouble winning Senate confirmation, though he had ruffled some feathers years before as the investigator of the Teapot Dome Scandal in the wake of the Harding Administration. "The genial and easily persuaded Roberts was highly sensitive to both personal and political pressure. Stung by collegial and public criticism of his opinions, he shifted them." On the Court he was often a swing vote. In some areas of law, however, he was comfortable and consistent, for example in his support for civil rights and his belief that the Fourteenth Amendment incorporated the Free Exercise Clause of the First Amendment and the right to an attorney. At the end of his career he finally grew into it. In the notorious *Korematsu v. U.S.* (1944), in which a majority of the Court upheld the forced relocation and internment of loyal Japanese American citizens, he dissented. Roberts no longer agreed with his brethren. "I dissent, because I think the indisputable facts exhibit a clear violation of Constitutional rights." He found that relocation on the basis of ancestry, as opposed to the curfew, was a clear violation of the Constitution. "It is the case of convicting a citizen as a punishment for not submitting to imprisonment in a concentration camp, based on his ancestry, and solely because of his ancestry, without evidence or inquiry concerning his loyalty and good disposition towards the United States." He retired in 1945, became dean of the University of Pennsylvania Law School, and died in 1955.[21]

Justice Harlan Fiske Stone dissented in *Butler*, joined by Justices Louis Brandeis and Benjamin Cardozo. Stone, a realist (someone who believed that law reflected real-life needs rather than abstract ideas) when he taught at Columbia Law School and generally a liberal on the Court, thought the time was ripe for the Court to take itself out of the business of overturning the people's will. "As the present depressed state of agriculture is nation wide in its extent and effects, there is no basis for saying that the expenditure of public money in aid of farmers is not within the specifically granted power of Congress to levy taxes to 'provide for the...general welfare.'" He did not cite the Preamble, however. Story's unilateral statement that the Preamble was unenforceable, adopted by the Supreme Court in 1906, constrained Stone.[22]

Scholars dispute whether the Court hears the voice of popular opinion, follows the election returns, or reads the newspapers. Prior to 1936, the United States Supreme Court uniformly heeded Madison's and Story's interpretation of the General Welfare Clause on the cases of federal regulations, sometimes citing them as authority on the proper construction of the General Welfare Clauses. After Roosevelt's overwhelming victory at the polls in 1936, one member of the Court changed his vote, and the Second New Deal programs were found constitutional. With that, the Preamble's broad language would be rehabilitated as constitutional law.[23]

The National Recovery Act and the Agricultural Adjustment Act were products of the first New Deal, temporary measures to achieve economic recovery, and while their demise was lamented by Cummings, Wallace, and Roosevelt, the second New Deal's package of legislation was more important to all three men. For "even in the heady moments of early 1937 [after the electoral victory of 1936] a quaver of foreboding crept into the president's celebration of economic recovery. His agenda had from the outset embraced more than simply restoring the economy to good health. He also aimed to enact durable reforms, to reshape the topography of American economic and social life." But all of these aims might be negated by an unfriendly Supreme Court majority.[24]

The most important of the second wave of statutes in terms of general welfare was the Social Security Act of 1935, sometimes called the Old Age Pension Act. The act created the Social Security Administration and, most importantly, a comprehensive system of pensions for those who had contributed into it. Contributions were compulsory from potential beneficiaries and from their employers. Thus it claimed to be a tax imposed for the general welfare. "An act to provide for the general welfare by establishing a system of Federal old-age benefits, and by enabling the several States to make more adequate provision for aged persons, blind persons, dependent and crippled children, maternal and child welfare, public health, and the administration of their unemployment compensation laws; to establish a Social Security Board; to raise revenue; and for other purposes." To raise the revenue for the program, "In addition to other taxes, there shall be levied, collected, and paid upon the income of every individual a tax" added to which "every employer shall pay an excise tax, with respect to having individuals in his employ" according to schedules fixed in the legislation. The act did not change the distribution of wealth very much, or the laborer–employer relation, or imperil the capitalist system of free enterprise. It simply imposed a tax on workers and employers to provide a public version of a pension plan. In this sense, it captured the essence of the Preamble— everyone had a stake in the general welfare of the elderly worker; it was simple justice for employer and employee to contribute to that stake.[25]

The act was controversial from its inception, critics denouncing it as a form of socialism. Its sponsors defended it as merely a form of insurance to which workers and employers paid premiums. As the inevitable legal challenge to the act moved from the steps of the High Court's "Marble Palace" to its red-curtained inner chamber, one correspondent to the *Washington Post* urged "lawyers whose opinions are not swayed by fat salaries from still fatter corporations" to save laws that "forbid starvation" of the elderly work force. Meanwhile, the U.S. Chamber of Commerce and the National Association of Manufacturers, representing the larger employers, mounted a campaign to overturn the law.[26]

The challenge to the statute arrived at the Court in *Stewart Sewing Machine v. Davis* (1937), and Justice Cardozo delivered the

opinion of the Court, this time with Roberts joining the majority in support of the government and the statute. Cardozo, as was
his wont, wrote with precision and style. He found the meaning
of Congress's taxation power by analogy to the state constitutions,
a method almost eerily similar to the way in which the framers
constructed the federal Constitution. In 1787, the delegates based
much of their suggestions for the new government's form and powers on their own states' constitutions. The language of the Preamble
derived in part from the same sources. (One should note that Cardozo was for many years the chief justice of the New York State
Court of Appeals.) He wrote: "The subject matter of taxation open
to the power of the Congress is as comprehensive as that open to
the power of the states, though the method of apportionment may
at times be different." In fact, "The statute books of the states are
strewn with illustrations of taxes laid on occupations pursued of
common right. We find no basis for holding that the power in that
regard which belongs by accepted practice to the legislatures of the
states, has been denied by the Constitution to the Congress of the
nation." The tax was uniform, it applied throughout the nation, and
its purpose was clearly within the purview of Congress. Cardozo
waved away the well-rehearsed argument that the taxing power was
limited to the federal government's own debt with a citation to the
portion of Roberts' *Butler* opinion that mentioned Hamilton. Cardozo thus turned the argument against a broad General Welfare
Clause on its head, arguing that the nationwide insurance plan was
a narrow one because it nicely fit the confines of "promotion of the
general welfare." Here, quietly, without actually citing the Constitution, he inserted the Preamble's General Welfare Clause back into
the enacting portion of the Constitution. Nothing in the Taxation
Clause of Article I, Section 8, said "*promotion* of the general welfare."
It only said "to *provide*...for the general welfare" [italics added].[27]

In more recent years, the scope of permissible congressional
activity in aid of the general welfare has waxed and waned. In the
hands of fiscal and social conservatives the doctrine of "New federalism" has limited the reach of Congress. But the "safety net" that the
second New Deal placed beneath the feet of Americans remains in
place. While that network of unemployment and health insurance,
old-age pensions and social service programs is not itself safe against
privatization initiatives nor fiscal retrenchment, drastic reduction of

federal aid to the needy, old, and sick is not likely. The only certainty in constitutional history is the certainty of change.[28]

.................

The Civil War exigencies added to the Reconstruction Amendments placed heavier burdens on the authorities in Washington, D.C., as did successive waves of regulatory reform, including federal entitlements like Social Security and Medicare. "We the People" undertook these as a national burden, forming a more perfect union. Though the Preamble's promises of the blessings of liberty, justice, and the general welfare were not always explicitly cited in aid of an expanded role for the federal government, their direction was surely the one to which the Preamble pointed. The movement for equality of the races relied upon those promises. In the process, the language of the preamble once again truly belonged to We the People, not just to lawyers and the judges. As Martin Luther King declaimed in *Why We Can't Wait* (1964), the Civil Rights movement was "the resumption of that noble journey reflected in the preamble to the Constitution." Evolving in these ways, the Preamble continues to fulfill its final promise to enable a constitution for "our posterity."[29]

# "Our Posterity"

B y adding "our posterity" to the Preamble the framers imposed their ideal of law on generations to come. Much changed in American society over the course of those generations. Slavery ended, and men and women previously excluded from the blessings of liberty gained some portion of them. The Preamble helped each generation to re-envision the fundamental law, sometimes by changing it through amendment and more often through revised readings of the meaning of law. If the body of the "Constitution entrenches institutions and principles against reform" the Preamble looked ahead and beyond the enabling clauses in the Articles proper, for "Americans insisted that even after the creation of constitutions, the people had a role to play as the ruler." As Justice Stephen Breyer wrote in defending a racial imbalance remedy, in 2007, "The Founders meant the Constitution as a practical document that would transmit its basic values to future generations through principles that remained workable over time." Reference to the Preamble insured that the Constitution remained a living document.[1]

Whether enforceable or not, the Preamble is a vital part of our constitutional heritage. It too is a living document. When the statute law and the courts seem to afford no relief to the oppressed, the Preamble offers hope. As Franklin D. Roosevelt told the U.S. Congress on January 3, 1940, at a moment in our history when the lawless forces of tyranny and oppression seemed everywhere triumphant, "It was with far-sighted wisdom that the framers of our Constitution brought together in one magnificent phrase three great concepts—"common defense," "general welfare," and "domestic tranquility." Within a more perfect Union they held out the promise of justice and liberty to all Americans.[2]

It was not until the era of Civil Rights that a president explicitly recognized that the Preamble and separate-but-equal could not co-exist. When he signed the Civil Rights Act of 1964, President Lyndon B. Johnson told a national television audience, "We believe all men are entitled to the blessings of liberty, yet millions are being deprived of those blessings—not because of their own failures, but because of the color of their skins.... [It] cannot continue."[3]

When New Jersey's Peter Rodino retired from Congress, he accepted a post at Seton Hall Law School in Newark, New Jersey. In his years there, he proposed a vibrant reading of the Preamble. As a lawyer and long-serving member of the House of Representatives, he knew that the potency of the Preamble had been drawn off by the courts. It was not a dead letter, but it had ceased to be law and had become a landmark of political rhetoric. He set about challenging that. In the Preamble he found "the aspiring goals of Americans." Those goals were a liberating force from superstition and oppression.[4]

Over the generations Americans found that the same words reflected larger and more inclusive goals, including the empowerment of minorities and women. As Justice Hugo Black explained his concurrence in a case of police misconduct, jailing civil rights marchers in Chicago when they had merely peaceably assembled, "This I think this is a highly important case which requires more detailed consideration than the Court's opinion gives it. It in a way tests the ability of the United States to keep the promises its Constitution makes to the people of the nation. Among those promises appearing in the preamble to the Constitution are the statements that the people of the United States ordained this basic charter... 'to secure the blessings of liberty to ourselves and our posterity.'"[5]

The controversy over the role of preambles in the federal Constitution continues. In two cases involving local gun-control ordinances, *District of Columbia v. Heller* (2008) and *McDonald v. City of Chicago* (2010), the role of a preamble moved front and center. The question was whether the preamble to the Second Amendment, "A well regulated militia being necessary to the security of a free State" limited "the right of the People to keep and bear arms" which the amendment guaranteed "shall not be infringed." Proponents of the "collective" theory of gun control argued that the preamble allowed the federal government and the state governments to regulate gun ownership and the bearing of those weapons in public. Proponents of the "individual right" theory countered that the preamble was only a statement of general principles and did not constrain the enforcing clause. In *Heller* Justice Antonin Scalia, quoting Justice George Sutherland, found that "in America 'the settled principle of law is that the preamble cannot control the enacting part of the statute in cases where the enacting part is expressed in clear, unambiguous terms.'" Presumably this meant that the first clause was a preamble, and as such it did not control the enacting clause (though the Court did concede that some gun control regulations might be permissible). If, however, one recognizes that the Bill of Rights does in fact constitute ten amendments to the Constitution, and the Constitution already has a Preamble, then the first part of the Amendment is just that—not a preamble but merely the first of the two clauses that comprise the Amendment. In all, the controversy led to hundreds of thousands of words in law review journals and threw no new light on whether preambles were part of laws or ancillary to them when the enacting part was not so clear.[6]

Despite the Court's refusal to find its clauses self-executing, the Preamble's underlying formula has found its way into all the legal forums where Americans talk about themselves and tell themselves who they are. The notion of perfecting the Union, incorporating in its capacious language the other clauses of the Preamble, has made those lines more than mere purposive phrasing. It has proved itself a shorthand for the nation's highest ideals—the goals that Roosevelt pledged the United States to exemplify, that Justice Black invoked, and Congressman Rodino celebrated. As presidential candidate Barack Obama told an audience in 2008, "a Constitution that promised its people liberty, and justice, and union that could be and should be perfected over time" was a Constitution worthy of a great nation. In this sense, the constraints that some jurists have placed on the Preamble do not capture its history or constrain its continuing ability to inspire us. Instead, the ongoing recovery of its contested meanings is the real story of the Preamble.[7]

A final thought: Obama is a lawyer, and his vision of the Preamble, though not the same as Morris's, Hamilton's, and the other framer-lawyers, carries on in their tradition. The Constitution in their hands was always a living thing. It still is.

# NOTES

........................

**Introduction**

1. Webster, quoted in Joshua C. Kendall, *The Forgotten Founding Father: Noah Webster's Obsession and the Creation of an American Culture* (New York: Putnam, 2011), 190; Kemble, quoted in Elizabeth Fox-Genovese and Eugene Genovese, *Mind of the Master Class* (New York: Cambridge University Press, 2005), 342; John Hope Franklin, *A Southern Odyssey: Travelers in the Antebellum North* (Baton Rouge: Louisiana State University Press, 1977), 202 ("down the stream of vice"); Margaret Coit, *John C. Calhoun, An American Portrait* (Columbia: University of South Carolina Press, 1950), 291.

2. Terry Bouton, *Taming Democracy: "The People," The Founders, and the Troubled End of the Revolution* (New York: Oxford University Press, 2009), 4; Susan B. Anthony, speech at National Women's Suffrage Association convention on January 16, 1873, in Ann D. Gordon, ed., *The Selected Papers of Elizabeth Cady Stanton and Susan B. Anthony, Vol. II: Against the Aristocracy of Sex, 1866–1873* (New Brunswick, NJ: Rutgers University Press, 2000), 556. Reference (along with so much else) courtesy of N. E. H. Hull. The subject of the blind spots of the framers is one that has and will trouble scholars so long as the framers interest historians. See Alan Gibson, *Interpreting the Founding: Guide to the Enduring Debates over the Origins and Foundations of the American Republic* 2nd ed. (Lawrence: University Press of Kansas, 2009), 134–140.

3. Jon Butler, *Becoming America: The Revolution before 1776* (Cambridge, MA: Harvard University Press, 2000), 247; Daniel Boorstin, *The Americans: The National Experience* (New York: Random House, 1965), 292.

4. Edward A. Purcell, *Originalism, Federalism, and the American Constitutional Enterprise: A Historical Inquiry* (New Haven, CT: Yale University Press, 2007), 176. The distinctions among original meaning and original intent are teased out in Jack Rakove, *Original Meanings: Politics and Ideas in the Making of the*

*Constitution* (New York: Knopf, 1996), 7–8. Jurisprudential originalism is the doctrine of constitutional interpretation bidding that the judge look to the intent of the framers as the guide to the application of constitutional language. "Courts should accordingly determine how the provisions were understood at the time they were ratified, and that understanding should guide decisions." The judge's reading of that intent dictates his opinion in constitutional litigation. Originalism not only assumes an objectivity that would make most working historians uncomfortable, it assumes a level of confidence in the historical findings that historians themselves would not share. In short, as a mode of constitutional interpretation, originalism is not very historical. James E. Ryan, "Does It Take a Theory? Originalism, Active Liberty, and Minimalism" *Stanford Law Review* 58 (March 2006), 1264. In 1985 Attorney General Edwin Meese's call for a "jurisprudence of original intent" before the American Bar Association was rebutted by Justice William Brennan's call for a living Constitution in a speech at Georgetown Law School. A "new originalism" has since emerged, relying less on the specific intent of the framers and instead on the plain meaning of the language at the time it was written. Justice Antonin Scalia has called this the basis for a "rock-solid, unchanging Constitution," a conclusion that the continuing debates over the history and the doctrine do little to support. Stephen G. Calabresi, in Antonin Scalia and Stephen G. Calabresi, eds., *Originalism: A Quarter Century of Debate* (New York: Regnery, 2007), 1; Antonin Scalia, *A Matter of Interpretation: Federal Courts and the Law* (Princeton: Princeton University Press, 1997), 47. On the Meese–Brennan exchange, see Seth Stern and Stephen Wermiel, *Justice Brennan: Liberal Champion* (New York: Houghton Mifflin, 2010), 504–506. Both of the speeches appear in Scalia and Calabresi, eds., *Originalism: A Quarter Century of Debate*, 47–71. On the "new originalism" and its problems, see Mark Tushnet, "*Heller* and the New Originalism," 69 *Ohio State Law Journal* (2008), 609–610 and R. B. Bernstein, "The Constitution as an Exploding Cigar and other 'Historians' Heresies' About a Constitutional Orthodoxy" *New York Law Review* 55 (2010/2011), 1073–1095.

5. Pauline Maier, *American Scripture: Making the Declaration of Independence* (New York: Vintage, 1997), xvi.

6. See, generally, Richard E. Labrunski, *James Madison and the Struggle for the Bill of Rights* (New York: Oxford University Press, 2006).

7. For an intriguing list of these preambles, see Eugene Volokh, "The Commonplace Second Amendment" *New York University Law Review* 73 (1998), 814.

## Prologue

1. John R. Vile, *The Constitutional Convention of 1787: A Comprehensive Encyclopedia of America's Founding* (New York: ABC-Clio, 2005), 2:424.

2. Laurel Thatcher Ulrich, *The Age of Homespun: Objects and Stories in the Creation of An American Myth* (New York: Knopf, 2001), 301; Wendy Gamber, *The Boarding House in Nineteenth Century America* (Baltimore: Johns Hopkins University Press, 2007), 92, 93; Frances Trollope, *Domestic Manners of the Americans* (London, 1832), 1:36–37; George Washington, "Rules of Civility…A Book of Etiquette" ([1774] reprinted Williamsburg, VA: Beaver Press, 1971).

3. Ron Chernow, *Alexander Hamilton* (New York: Penguin, 2004), 5, 17; Julius H. Goebel, ed., *The Law Practice of Alexander Hamilton* (New York: Columbia University Press, 1964), 1: 48–49.

4. Woody Holton, *Unruly Americans and the Origins of the Constitution* (New York: Hill and Wang, 2007), 194; James J. Kirsche, *Gouverneur Morris: Author, Statesman, and Man of the World* (New York: St. Martins, 2005), 265.

5. Kirsche, *Morris*, 121.

6. David O. Stewart, *The Summer of 1787: The Men Who Invented the Constitution* (New York: Simon and Schuster, 2007), 35; Richard Beeman, *Plain, Honest Men: The Making of the American Constitution* (New York: Random House, 2009), 204; Carol Berkin, *A Brilliant Solution: Inventing the American Constitution* (New York: Houghton Mifflin, 2003), 53.

7. James Madison to Jared Sparks, April 8, 1831, in Max Farrand, ed., *Records of the Federal Constitutional Convention* (New Haven: Yale University Press, 1911), 3:500.

## Chapter One

1. Joseph Ellis, *American Creation: The Triumphs and Tragedies at the Founding of the Republic* (New York: Knopf, 2008), 61.

2. Kirsche, *Morris*, 23–25, 26, 28.

3. George Washington to Continental Congress, December 23, 1777, in W. C. Ford, ed., *The Writings of George Washington* (New York: Putnam, 1889–1893), 6:257. Washington did exaggerate a bit to compel Congress to pay attention. See Wayne K. Bodle, *The Valley Forge Winter: Civilians and Soldiers in War* (State College, PA: Pennsylvania State University Press, 2004), 168–169.

4. Here and after, Gouverneur Morris to John Jay, February 1, 1778, *The Life of Gouverneur Morris, With Selections from His Correspondence*, ed. Jared Sparks (Boston: Gray, 1832), 1:153. See also William Howard Adams, *Gouverneur Morris: An Independent Life* (New Haven: Yale University Press, 2003), 97; Charles Royster, *A Revolutionary People at War: The Continental Army and American Character, 1775–1783* (Chapel Hill: University of North Carolina Press, 1980), 358.

5. Here and after, text adapted from Peter Charles Hoffer, *Law and People in Colonial America* 2nd ed. (Baltimore: Johns Hopkins University Press, 1998), 127–132. A recent major study of colonial law has argued that it had little to do with law in the early nation. See G. Edward White, *Law in American History, Volume 1: From the Colonial Period to the Civil War* (New York: Oxford University Press, 2012), 489–490 n. 45. In fact, colonial law practitioners like Morris, Adams, and Jefferson were the framers of early national law, and refashioned the thinking of colonial constitutionalism to create the state and federal constitutions. One finds strong continuities between the two periods rather than discontinuity.

6. The (alleged) conspiracy against liberty is unraveled in Bernard Bailyn, *The Ideological Origins of the American Revolution*, enlarged edition (Cambridge, MA: Harvard University Press, 1992), 119 and after.

7. John Fabian Witt, *Patriots and Cosmopolitans: Hidden Histories of American Law* (Cambridge, MA: Harvard University Press, 2007), 76.

8. Wilson's unpublished address appears in James Wilson, "Considerations on Parliament" [1768], in Robert McCloskey, ed., *Works of James Wilson* (Cambridge, MA, 1967), 2:734, 735.

9. Thanks for this way of seeing Wilson's contribution go to Kunal Parker, *Common Law, History and Democracy in America, 1790–1900: Legal Thought Before Modernism* (New York: Cambridge University Press, 2011), 65.

10. Wilson's speech to the Pennsylvania assembly is reprinted in McCloskey, ed., *Works of Wilson*, 2: 747–758. For the older sense of liberty as freedom from illegal arrest or other restraint, see William Blackstone, *Commentaries on the Laws of England* (1765), 1:134.

11. Gordon S. Wood, *The Americanization of Benjamin Franklin* (New York: Penguin, 2005), 145–146; Walter Isaacson, *Benjamin Franklin: An American Life* (New York: Simon and Schuster, 2003), 308.

12. Joseph Ellis, *Passionate Sage: The Character and Legacy of John Adams* (New York: Norton, 1992), 37; Ellis, *American Creation*, 25.

13. John Adams, September 15, 1775, in *The Diary and Autobiography of John Adams*, eds. Lyman Butterfield et al. (Cambridge, MA: Harvard University Press, 1961 ), 2:173; Berkin, *Brilliant Solution*, 212.

14. George Dangerfield, *Chancellor Robert R. Livingston of New York, 1743–1813* (New York: Harcourt, Brace, 1960), 79–82.

15. Virginia Scharff, *The Women Jefferson Loved* (New York: Harper, 2010), 153.

16. Joseph J. Ellis, *American Sphinx: The Character of Thomas Jefferson* (New York: Knopf, 1997), 12; R. B. Bernstein, *Thomas Jefferson* (New York: Oxford University Press, 2004), xii.

17. Thomas Jefferson, "Declaration of the Causes and Necessity of Taking Up Arms" 1775, *Papers of Thomas Jefferson* eds. Julian P. Boyd et al. (Princeton, NJ: Princeton University Press, 1950–), 1:187–209.

18. Jay Fliegelman, *Declaring Independence: Jefferson, Natural Language, and the Culture of Performance* (Stanford: Stanford University Press, 1992), 64 (Jefferson wrote as the voice of the people).

19. Thomas Jefferson, *The Autobiography of Thomas Jefferson* [1823] (Richmond, VA: Taylor and Maury, 1853), 7.

20. Thomas Jefferson to Edward Carrington, January 16, 1787 *Writings of Thomas Jefferson* ed. Paul L. Ford (New York: Putnam, 1894), 4:357.

21. On the Jefferson–Mason collaboration, see Jeff Broadwater, *George Mason: Forgotten Founder* (Charlottesville: University of Virginia Press, 2009), 276 n.56; on Mason and slavery, ibid., 14, 33–36, 194.

22. Quoted in Merrill Jensen, *The American Revolution Within America* (New York: New York University Press, 1974), 86; Pennsylvania Const. of 1776.

23. Jack N. Rakove, *James Madison and the Creation of the American Republic* 2nd ed. (New York: Longman, 2002), 4, 15.

24. Robert Ernst, *Rufus King, American Federalist* (Chapel Hill: University of North Carolina Press, 1968), 92–93, 117; Richard E. Welch, Jr., "Rufus King of Newburyport: The Formative Years" *Essex Institute Historical Collections* 96 (October 1960), 245.

25. Ernst, *King*, 29; Benjamin Woods Labaree, *Patriots and Partisans: The Merchants of Newburyport, 1764–1815* (Cambridge, MA: Harvard University Press, 1962), 55. Oscar Handlin and Mary Flug Handlin, eds., *The Popular Sources of Political Authority: Documents on the Massachusetts Constitution of 1780* (Cambridge, MA: Harvard University Press, 1966), 25–26, 319–320.

26. *The Constitution of the State of Massachusetts, Adopted 1780, With the Amendments Annexed* (Boston: Richardson and Lord, 1826), 3. On Adams' *Thoughts on Government* (1776), see John Ferling, *John Adams: A Life* (New York: Oxford University Press, 2010), 155–156.

27. *The Life and Correspondence of Rufus King*, ed. Charles R. King (New York: Putnam, 1894–1900), 1:39

28. New York State Constitution of 1777, April, 20, 1777, *Journals of the Provincial Congress, Provincial Convention Committee of Safety and Council of Safety of the State of New York, 1775, 1776, 1777* (Albany, NY: Thurlow Weed, 1842) 1: 892–898.

29. Kirsche, *Morris*, 295.

30. See, e.g., Terry Bouton, "Moneyless in Pennsylvania: Privatization and the Depression of the 1780s" in Cathy Matson, ed., *The Economy of Early America: Historical Perspectives and New Directions* (Philadelphia: University of Pennsylvania Press, 2007), 221.

31. Benjamin Franklin to Henry Laurens, May 25, 1782, in *Papers of Benjamin Franklin*, ed. Leonard W. Labaree (New Haven: Yale University Press, 1960), 37:415: John Jay to William Livingston, July 19, 1783, in *John Jay: The Winning of the Peace, Unpublished Papers, 1780–1784* ed. Richard B. Morris (New York: Harper, 1980), 564. On the travails of the diplomats in the confederation era, see Reginald Horsman, *The Diplomacy of the New Republic, 1776–1815* (Arlington Heights, IL: Davidson, 1985), 28–41.

32. James Wilson, *Considerations on the Bank of North America"* [1785] reprinted in *Works of James Wilson*, ed. James DeWitt Andrews (Chicago: Callaghan, 1898), 558.

33. Jack P. Greene, "The Background of the Articles of Confederation" in Peter Onuf, ed., *Congress and the Confederation* (New York: Harpers, 1991), 42–43; Jerrilyn Greene Marston, *King and Congress: The Transfer of Political Legitimacy, 1774–1776* (Princeton: Princeton University Press, 1987), 299–304 (Congress replaced the king, not Parliament); Jack Rakove, *The Beginnings of National Politics: An Interpretive History of the Continental Congress* (Baltimore: Johns Hopkins University Press, 1979), 29.

34. Jerry W. Markham, *A Financial History of the United States* (Armonk, NY: Sharpe, 2002), 3:112.

35. Peter Onuf, *Statehood and Union: A History of the Northwest Ordinance* (Bloomington: Indiana University Press, 1987), 42–43; Onuf, *The Origins of the Federal Republic: Jurisdictional Controversies in the United States, 1775–1787* (Philadelphia: University of Pennsylvania Press, 1983), 161–162.

36. Continental Congress, 7 Aug. 1786 *Journals of the Continental Congress* (Washington, DC: U.S. Government Printing Office, 1904–1937), 31:494–498: "The Grand Committee consisting of Mr. [Samuel] Livermore, Mr. [Nathan] Dane, Mr. [James] Manning, Mr. [William Samuel] Johnson, Mr. [Melancton] Smith, Mr. [John Cleves] Symmes, Mr. [Charles] Pettit, Mr. [William] Henry, Mr. [Henry] Lee, Mr. [Timothy] Bloodworth, Mr. [Charles] Pinckney and Mr. [William] Houstoun appointed to report such amendments to the confederation, and such resolutions as it may be necessary to recommend to the several states for the purpose of obtaining from them such powers as will render the federal government adequate to the ends for which it was instituted"; Mass. Const. Preamble [1780]; Pauline Maier, *Ratification: The People Debate the Constitution, 1787–1788* (New York: Simon and Schuster, 2010), 140.

37. Onuf, *Origins of the Federal Republic*, 91 and after; George Mason to Thomas Jefferson, September 27, 1781, *Papers of Thomas Jefferson*, 2: 697–698.

38. Chernow, *Alexander Hamilton*, 222; Ralph L. Ketcham, *James Madison: A Biography* (Charlottesville, VA: University of Virginia Press, 1990), 185.

39. Report of the Commissioners, Annapolis, Md., September 14, 1786, usconstitution.net/annapolis.html.

40. Madison to Edmund Pendleton, February 24, 1787 *The Writings of James Madison*, ed. Gaillard Hunt (New York: Putnam, 1902) 2:318–319; Madison to George Washington, April 16, 1787, *Papers of James Madison*, M. E. Rachel et al., eds. (Chicago: University of Chicago Press, 1975), 9:382. On Madison as nationalist see Lance Banning, *The Sacred Fire of Liberty: James Madison and the Founding of the Federal Republic* (Ithaca, NY: Cornell University Press, 1995), 14–15.

41. David Szatmary, *Shays' Rebellion: The Making of an Agrarian Insurrection* (Amherst: University of Massachusetts Press, 1980), 125.

42. Merrill Jensen, *The Articles of Confederation: An Interpretation of the Social-constitutional History of the American Revolution, 1774–1781* (Madison: University of Wisconsin Press, 1959), 8 and after; Jackson Turner Main and Edward Countryman, *The Antifederalists: Critics of the Constitution, 1781–1788*, rev. ed. (Chapel Hill: University of North Carolina Press, 2004), 261.

43. Richard D. Brown, "Shays's Rebellion and the Ratification of the Federal Constitution in Massachusetts" in Richard Beeman, Stephen Botein, and Edward C. Carter III, eds., *Beyond Confederation: Origins of the Constitution and American National Identity* (Chapel Hill: University of North Carolina Press, 1987), 117; see also, generally, Leonard L. Richards, *Shays's Rebellion: The American Revolution's Final Battle* (Philadelphia: University of Pennsylvania Press, 2004).

44. James Bowdoin, *To the Commonwealth of Massachusetts, A Proclamation*, September 2, 1786 (Boston: Adams and Nourse, 1786), n.p.; George Washington to Henry Lee, October 31, 1786, *Writings of George Washington*, ed. James C. Fitzpatrick (Charlottesville: University of Virginia Press, 1931–1944), 29: 34. See generally Gordon Wood, *Creation of the American Republic, 1776–1787* (Chapel Hill: University of North Carolina Press, 1969), 412–413.

45. Journal of the Continental Congress, February 21, 1787, in Farrand, ed., *Records*, 3: 13.

## Chapter Two

1. Thomas Jefferson to John Adams, August 30, 1787; Ford, ed., *Works of Thomas Jefferson*, 5: 906; Bernstein, *Jefferson*, 114 ("envy").

2. Beeman, *Plain, Honest Men*, 24–25.

3. Rakove, *Original Meanings*, 55; Rakove, *Madison*, 61.

4. Joseph Ellis, *His Excellency: George Washington* (New York: Knopf, 2005), 172–178.

5. James Madison to Thomas Jefferson, May 15, 1787, in Farrand, ed., *Records* 3:20; Rakove, *Madison*, 62.

6. John R. Vile, ed., *The Constituitonal Convention of 1787: A Comprehensive Encyclopedia of America's Founding* (New York: ABC-Clio, 2005), 2:340; Beeman, *Plain, Honest Men*, 165; Forrest McDonald, *Alexander Hamilton: A Biography* (New York: Norton, 1982), 5.

7. Andrew Burstein and Nancy Isenberg, *Madison and Jefferson* (New York: Random House, 2010), 144.

8. Madison, Federalist No. 37 in *The Federalist*, ed. J. R. Pole (Indianapolis: Hackett, 2005), 193.

9. Madison to Edmund Pendleton, February 24, 1787, *The Writings of James Madison*, 2:318–319; Madison to George Washington, April 16, 1787, *Papers of James Madison*, 9:382; Banning, *The Sacred Fire of Liberty*, 14–15.

10. May 30, 1787, in Farrand, ed., *Records*, 1:27, 28, 33.

11. May 30, 1787, in Farrand, ed., *Records*, 1:34.

12. June 13, 1787, in Farrand, ed., *Records*, 1:225; June 15, 1787, in Farrand, ed., *Records*, 1:242.

13. John Philip Reid, *The Concept of Representation in the Age of the American Revolution* (Chicago: University of Chicago Press, 1988), 11, 28, 36, 98; Gordon S. Wood, *The Radicalism of the American Revolution* (New York: Knopf, 1992), 13, 57. I have borrowed the notion of keywords from Daniel Rogers, *Contested Truths: Keywords in American Politics* (New York: Basic Books, 1987), 60.

14. Charles Warren, *Congress, the Constitution, and the Supreme Court* (Boston: Little, Brown, 1935), 6–7; John Adams, *A Defense of the Constitutions of Government of the United States of America* (London: Stockdale, 1787), 153, 154; James Madison, Federalist No. 46, in Pole, ed., *The Federalist*, 261; Edward Everett, "Eulogy on Lafayette…September 6, 1834, Everett, *Orations and Speeches on Various Occasions* (Boston: American Stationers, 1836), 488.

15. Thomas W. Perry, *Public Opinion, Propaganda, and Politics in Eighteenth-Century England* (Cambridge, MA: Harvard University Press, 1962), 183; Bernard Bailyn, *To Begin the World Anew: The Genius and Ingenuity of the American Founders* (New York: Random House, 2004), 118.

16. George Washington, "Farewell Address," September 17, 1796, in James D. Richardson, ed., *A Compilation of the Messages and Papers of the Presidents* (Washington, D.C.: Bureau of National Literature and Art, 1908), 1: 275.

17. Madison, Federalist No. 10, in Pole, ed., *The Federalist*, 48.

18. Hamilton, Federalist No. 26, in Pole, ed., *The Federalist*, 138.

19. Chernow, *Hamilton*, 235.

20. Here and after, Alexander Hamilton, June 18, 1787, in Farrand, ed., *Records*, 1:282–293.

21. Madison, Federalist No. 39, in Pole, ed., *The Federalist*, 207, 209; Beeman, *Plain, Honest Men*, 181–189, 221–224.

22. Madison, June 30, 1787, in Farrand, ed., *Records*, 1:485.

23. Douglas Ambrose and Robert W. T. Martin, eds., *The Many Faces of Alexander Hamilton: The Life and Legacy of America's Most Elusive Founder* (New York: New York University Press, 2006), 18; Henry Wiencek, *An Imperfect God: George Washington, His Slaves, and the Creation of America* (New York: Farrar, Strauss and Giroux, 2004), 390 n.20; Madison, Federalist No. 43, in Pole, ed., *The Federalist*, 239.

24. John Philip Reid, *The Concept of Liberty in the Age of the American Revolution* (Chicago: University of Chicago Press, 1988), 47–48; Paul Finkelman, *Slavery and the Founders: Race and Liberty in the Age of Jefferson* (Armonk, NY: M. E. Sharpe, 2001), 25.

25. Holton, *Unruly Americans*, 220–221. On slave rebellion, and fears of slave rebellion, see, e.g., Peter Charles Hoffer, *Cry Liberty: The Great Stono River Slave Rebellion of 1739* (New York: Oxford University Press, 2010), 56–57, and Hoffer, *The Great New York Conspiracy of 1741: Slavery, Crime, and Colonial Law* (Lawrence: University Press of Kansas, 2003), 48–49.

26. Holton, *Unruly Americans*, 221; Beeman, *Plain, Honest Men*, 309–310; Gary Nash, *Race and Revolution* (Lanham, MD: Rowman and Littlefield, 1990), 182.

27. James Wilson, June 11, 1787, in Farrand, ed., *Records*, 1:200. How central was slavery to the work of the convention, and by that logic, to the final structure and content of the Constitution? Finkelman, *Slavery and the Founders*, 5, argues that the accommodation with slavery in the Constitution was essential to the "creation of the Union." Without "the bargain" there would have been no union); David Waldstreicher, *Slavery's Constitution: From Revolution to Ratification* (New York: Hill and Wang, 2009), 17, writes "slavery was as important to the making of the Constitution as the Constitution was important to the survival of slavery," but Rakove, *Original Meanings*, 72, 73, finds that "the dominant view expressed by Northern delegates, however, accepted the accommodation with slavery as the price of union … the Three-Fifths Clause, then, was neither a coefficient of racial hierarchy nor a portent of the racialist thinking of the next century."

28. Stewart, *Summer of 1787*, 78.

29. Rufus King to Convention, August 8, 1787, in Farrand, ed., *Records*, 2:502; Gouverneur Morris to Convention, August 8, 1787, Farrand, ed., *Records*, 2:514.

30. Waldstreicher, *Slavery's Constitution*, 116–117; Hamilton to John Jay, March 14, 1779, Harold C. Syrett et al., eds., *The Papers of Alexander Hamilton* (New York: Columbia University Press, 1961–1979) 2: 18; John Jay to the President of the [English] Society for Promoting the

Manumission of Slaves, June 1788, *Correspondence of John Jay*, ed. Henry P. Johnson (New York: Putnam, 1890–1893), 3: 340, 344.

31. Here and after, Madison, Federalist No. 54, in Pole, ed., *The Federalist*, 295–298. He was familiar with the dialogue format; he learned it at college. Ketcham, *Madison*, 32. In Socratic dialogues, Socrates always won the day. In David Hume's discourse on religion (*Dialogues Concerning Natural Religion* [1779], prudently withheld from publication until he died, the atheist won. Here, the defense of the Three-Fifths Clause won.

## Chapter Three

1. September 8, 1787, debates, in Farrand, ed., *Records*, 2:553.
2. David Lieberman, "The Mixed Constitution and Common Law" in Mark Goldie and Robert Wokler, eds., *Cambridge History of Eighteenth-Century Thought* (Cambridge, Eng.: Cambridge University Press, 2006), 317; Alexander Hamilton, Federalist No. 6, in Pole, ed., *The Federalist*, 27; James Madison, Federalist No. 37, in ibid., 197.
3. Randolph, July 26, in Farrand, ed., *Records*; 2:137–138.
4. August 6, 1787, in Farrand, ed., *Records*, 2:137, 150, 152, 177; August 7, 1787, in Farrand, ed., *Records*, 2:196.
5. I am grateful to R. B. Bernstein for these thoughts on Article VII.
6. George C. Croce, Jr., *William Samuel Johnson: A Maker of the Constitution* (New York: Columbia University Press, 1937), 134.
7. Croce, *Johnson*, 141, 142–147; Stewart, *Summer of 1787*, 81–82 (Johnson diary); Beeman, *Plain, Honest Men*, 310 (household slaves).
8. Baldwin told as much to Ezra Stiles; see Farrand, ed., *Records*, 1:170; Farrand, ed., *Records*, 3:420 (Morris to Pickering, December 22, 1814); Farrand, ed., *Records*, 3:499 (Madison to Sparks, April 8, 1831).
9. Jennifer Nedelsky, *Private Property and the Limits of American Constitutionalism* (Chicago: University of Chicago Press, 1994), 67–68, 87.
10. I thank Jack Rakove for calling this text to my attention. My reading of it is not necessarily his.
11. September 4, 1787, Farrand, ed., *Records*, 2:493, 499; Beeman, *Plain, Honest Men*, 298; Stewart, *Summer of 1787*, 211; Adams, *Morris*, 309 n.24.
12. John Jay, Federalist No. 3, in Pole, ed., *The Federalist*, 16; Jay, Federalist No. 5, in ibid., 24.
13. Richard B. Morris, *John Jay: The Winning of the Peace* (New York: Harper, 1988), 8–10 and after; Casey White, *John Jay: Diplomat of the American Experiment* (New York: Rosen, 2006), 12.
14 Rufus King, June 19, 1787, in Farrand, ed., *Records*, 1:133; King, August 28, 1787, ibid, 2:220.
15. Pierce Butler, August 18, 1787, in Farrand, ed., *Records* 2:133.
16. Chisholm v. Georgia, 2 U.S. 419 , 475, 476 (1793) (Jay, C.J.).

17. Here and after Farrand, ed., *Records*, 2:583–584.
18. Madison, Federalist No. 10: "Complaints are every where heard from our most considerate and virtuous citizens, equally the friends of public and private faith, and of public and personal liberty, that our governments are too unstable, that the public good is disregarded in the conflicts of rival parties, and that measures are too often decided, not according to the rules of justice and the rights of the minor party, but by the superior force of an interested and overbearing majority.... The influence of factious leaders may kindle a flame within their particular States, but will be unable to spread a general conflagration through the other States." Pole, ed., *The Federalist*, 48.
19. James Wilson at the Pennsylvania Ratification convention, December 1, 1787, in John Bach McMaster and Frederick D. Stone, eds., *Pennsylvania and the Federal Constitution, 1787–1788* (Lancaster: Historical Society of Pennsylvania, 1888), 301.
20. Elbridge Gerry, "Hon. Mr. Gerry's Objections" October 18, 1787, reprinted in *Philadelphia Evening Herald* November 17, 1787, p. 353; Saul Cornell, *The Other Founders: Anti-Federalism and the Dissenting Tradition in America, 1788–1828* (Chapel Hill: University of North Carolina Press, 1999), 28; Edmund Randolph to James Madison, October 23, 1787, in Moncure D. Conway, *Omitted Chapters of History Disclosed in the Life and Papers of Edmund Randolph* (New York: Putnam, 1888), 95.
21. James Wilson's October 10, 1787, speech, reprinted in the newspapers, was the first publicized defense of the Constitution, but he was not the first to break the silence of the convention on the issues.
22. Richard Henry Lee to Edmund Randolph, December 6, 1787, in David J.Siemers, ed., *The Anti-Federalists* (Lanham, MD: Rowman and Littlefield, 2003), 103; Maier, *Ratification*, 52–53.
23. William Samuel Johnson, September 27, 1787, to Congress, in Merrill Jensen et al., eds., *Documentary History of the Ratification of the Constitution* (Madison: University of Wisconsin Press, 1976–), 1:339.
24. Madison, September 27, 1787, ibid., 1:339.
25. King, September 27, ibid., 1:340.
26. Gouverneur Morris to George Washington, October 30, 1787, *The Debates in the Several State Conventions*, ed. Jonathan Elliot (Washington, DC: U.S. Congress, 1836), 1:506.

**Chapter Four**
1. John Jay, Federalist No. 2, in Pole, ed., *The Federalist*, 6; Rakove, *Original Meanings*, 171.
2. Terry W. Lipscomb, "Introduction" in Lipscomb, ed., *The Letters of Piece Butler, 1790–1794* (Columbia, SC: University of South Carolina Press, 2007), xxix; Maier, *Ratification*, 64–65.

3. Cornell, *The Other Founders*, 307; Herbert W. Storing, *What the Anti-Federalists Were For: the Political Thought of the Opponents of the Constitution* (Chicago: University of Chicago Press, 1981), 11 and after.

4. Compare, for example, Cecelia Kenyon, "Men of Little Faith: The Antifederalists on the Nature of Representative Government" *William and Mary Quarterly* 3rd Ser. 12 (1955), 3–43 with Cornell, *The Other Founders*, and Woody Holton, *Unruly Americans*, with Forrest McDonald, *We the People: The Economic Origins of the Federal Constitution* (Chicago: University of Chicago Press, 1958).

5. Patrick Henry, *The Life, Correspondence, and Speeches of Patrick Henry*, ed. William Wirt Henry (New York: Scribner's, 1891), 3:433; Edmund Randolph, June 25, 1788, in *Documentary History of the Ratification of the Constitution*, 10:1532; George Wythe, June 24, 1788, ibid., 10: 1500–1501; George Nicholas, ibid., 10: 1506.

6. Alexander Hamilton, Federalist No. 84, in Pole, ed., *The Federalist*, 455.

7. Melancton Smith, June 20, 1788, in David Wooton, ed., *The Essential Federalist and Anti-Federalist Papers* (Indianapolis: Hackett, 2007), 42.

8. Maier, *Ratification*, 320–397; Beeman, *Plain, Honest Men*, 402.

9. Maier, *Ratification*, 84–85; Douglass Adair, "The Federalist Papers: A Review Essay" *William and Mary Quarterly* 3rd ser. 22 (1965), 133.

10. John Jay, Federalist No. 3, in Pole, ed., *The Federalist*, 9.

11. James Madison, Federalist No. 41, in Pole, ed., *The Federalist*, 220.

12. Alexander Hamilton, Federalist No. 8, in Pole, ed., *The Federalist*, 39; Hamilton, Federalist No. 29, in ibid., 152.

13. George Washington, "First Annual Message to Congress," January 8, 1790, in Richardson, ed., *Messages of the Presidents* 1:68.

14. George Washington, Proclamation of Neutrality, April 22, 1793; Editor's Introduction to "Outline for George Washington's Fifth Annual Address to Congress, November 1793," in Syrett et al., eds., *The Papers of Alexander Hamilton*, 15:426; and see Joseph Ellis, *Founding Brothers: The Revolutionary Generation* (New York: Knopf, 2000), 135, 151–154.

15. George Washington, "Farewell Address," September 17, 1796, in Richardson, ed., *Messages of the Presidents*, 1:275. On Hamilton's contribution, see Felix Gilbert, *The Beginnings of American Foreign Policy: To the Farewell Address* (Princeton: Princeton University Press, 1961), 125–140.

16. Carl Becker, "Constitutional Government," in Becker, *Freedom and Responsibility in the American Way of Life* (New York: Vintage, 1955), 81–82; Christopher Grasso, *A Speaking Aristocracy: Transforming Public Discourse in the Eighteenth Century* (Chapel Hill: University of North Carolina Press, 1999), 85 n.79.

17. On colonial and revolutionary law, see, e.g., Hoffer, *Law and People in Colonial America*, 47, 150; for the "Declaration of the Rights of Man and

of Citizens" August 26, 1789, Article 6, see Dale Van Kley, *The French Idea of Freedom* (Palo Alto: Stanford University Press, 1997), 2, 6 and after.

18. See, e.g., Richard Beeman, *The Varieties of Political Experience in Eighteenth-Century America* (Philadelphia: University of Pennsylvania Press, 1999), 92, 95, 103 (colonial patronage); J. G. A. Pocock, *Virtue, Commerce, and History* (New York: Cambridge University Press, 1976), 78 (British patronage practices); Wood, *Radicalism of the American Revolution*, 104 (devotion and sacrifice), 301 (patronage in the Federalist era).

19. Here and after, Alexander Hamilton, "Report on Manufactures" December 5, 1791, in Syrett et al., eds., *The Papers of Alexander Hamilton*, 10:302.

20. Madison, Federalist No. 41, in Pole, ed., *The Federalist*, 225. But taken together Hamilton's domestic program was the catalyst of the first national two-party system. Joseph Charles, *The Origins of the American Party System* (New York: Harper, 1961), 26–27.

21. James Madison, Federalist No. 41, in Pole, ed., *The Federalist*, 225; Ketcham, *Madison*, 332–333.

22. Forrest McDonald, *Alexander Hamilton: A Biography* (New York: Norton, 1982), 201–202, suggests that the disagreement over the reading of the Constitution in the first years of the federal government was not a matter of consistent ideology so much as differing political stances.

23. Thomas Jefferson, "Opinion on the Constitutionality of a National Bank," January 15, 1791, *Writings of Jefferson*, 5:286.

24. Wiencek, *An Imperfect God*, 100.

25. Here and after, George Washington, "Second Annual Address," December 8, 1790, in Richardson, ed., *Messages of the Presidents*, 1:82.

26. Ralph A. Rossum, *The Supreme Court and Tribal Gaming: California v. Cabazon Band of Mission Indians* (Lawrence: University Press of Kansas, 2010), 3–60 (evolution of Indian policy in the executive and judicial branches); Bernard W. Sheehan, *Seeds of Extinction: Jeffersonian Philanthropy and the American Indian* (rev. ed., Chapel Hill: University of North Carolina Press, 2010), 120 (formalities of international treaty making were observed, but in fact Indians were not treated as foreign nationals). But see Leonard J. Sadosky, *Revolutionary Negotiations: Indians, Empires, and Diplomats in the Founding of America* (Charlottesville: University of Virginia Press, 2009), arguing that diplomacy and diplomatic formalities remained the key to early national Indian policy.

27. Theodore H. Hass, *The Indian and the Law* (Washington, DC: U.S. Government Printing Office, 1949), 3; N. Bruce Duthu, *American Indians and the Law* (New York: Viking, 2008), 84–85.

28. George Washington, "Fourth Annual Message," November 6, 1792, Richardson, ed., *Messages of the Presidents*, 1:127.

29. George Washington, "Proclamation," August 11, 1794, Richarson, ed., *Messages of the Presidents*, 1:160–161; Washington, "Sixth Annual Report," November 19, 1794, ibid., 1:164; Thomas Slaughter, *The Whiskey Rebellion: Frontier Epilogue to the American Revolution* (New York: Oxford University Press, 1988), 78, 216.

30. Slaughter, *Whiskey Rebellion*, 227.

31. Quoted in George C. Herring, *From Colony to Superpower, U.S. Foreign Relations Since 1776* (New York: Oxford University Press, 2008), 78.

32. Harper's identity as the source of the quotation is revealed in Paul F. Boller and John George, *They Never Said It: A Book of Fake Quotes, Misquotes, and Misleading Attributions* (New York: Oxford University Press, 1990), 106.

33. William Stinchcomb, *The XYZ Affair* (Westport, CT: Greenwood, 1981).

34. David McCullough, *John Adams* (New York: Simon and Schuster, 2001), 504–506; Patrick J. Charles, "The Plenary Power and the Constitutionality of Ideological Exclusion," in *Texas Review of Law and Politics* 15 (2010), 91–101, 104–105 (common defense cited in congressional debates, *Annals of Congress* 8:1790, 1974, 1981, 1986 [1798]); Charles Lee, *Defence of the Alien and Sedition Laws: Shewing their Entire Consistency with the Constitution of the United States, and the Principles of Our Government: Addressed to the People of Virginia* (Philadelphia: Fenno, 1798); 6.

35. Sedition Act of 1798, 1 U.S. Stat. 596. This and the following text from Peter Charles Hoffer, *The Free Press Crisis of 1800: Thomas Cooper's Trial for Seditious Libel* (Lawrence: University Press of Kansas, 2011), 32–50.

36. Kentucky Resolves: *Writings of Jefferson*, 7:289–294; on the resolves as precedent for nullification see, e.g., William Freehling, *The Road to Disunion, I: 1776–1854* (New York: Oxford University Press, 1991), 254 and after.

37. Rakove, *Original Meanings*, 83; Madison, "Speech in Congress," February 8, 1791, quoted in Rakove, *Original Meanings*, 355. Madison's role in preparing the resolves is explored in Robert Allen Rutland et al., eds., *Papers of James Madison, Congressional Series* (Charlottesville: University of Virginia Press, 1991), 17:186–188.

38. Here and after, Madison, "Draft of the Virginia Resolves," in Ralph Ketcham, ed., *Selected Writings of James Madison* (Indianapolis: Hackett, 2006), 239–248.

39. Madison, Federalist No. 39, in Pole, ed., *The Federalist*, 208; Madison, Federalist No. 46, in ibid., 225.

40. Washington to Adams, July 13, 1798, quoted in Martin N. Rosenfeld, *American Aurora* (New York: St. Martin's, 1997), 189.

41. Here and after, Madison, "Report of the Committee," *Letters and Other Writings of James Madison* (Philadelphia: Lippincott, 1865) 4:540–547. Compare Madison, Federalist No. 39: "The proposed Constitution

therefore is in strictness neither a national nor a federal constitution; but a composition of both. In its foundation, it is federal, not national; in the sources from which the ordinary powers of the Government are drawn, it is partly federal, and partly national: in the operation of these powers, it is national, not federal." Pole, ed., *The Federalist*, 211.

## Chapter Five

1. The description is taken from Peter Charles Hoffer, Williamjames H. Hoffer, and N. E. H. Hull, *The Supreme Court: An Essential History* (Lawrence: University Press of Kansas, 2007), 51.

2. James F. Simon, *What Kind of Nation: Thomas Jefferson, John Marshall, and the Epic Struggle to Create a United States* (New York: Simon and Schuster, 2003), 274; *McCulloch v. Maryland* 17 U.S. 316, 404 (1819) (Marshall, C. J.).

3. [Marshall] "A Friend of the Constitution" *Alexandria [Virginia] Gazette* July 15, 1819.

4. John C. Calhoun, Speech, February 2, 1817, *The Early American Republic: A Documentary Reader*, ed. Sean Patrick Adams (Hoboken: Wiley-Blackwell, 2008), 69; Henry Clay, Speech, February 4, 1817, Clay, "Speech on the Land Act of 1833," in *Life, Correspondence, and Speeches of of Henry Clay*, ed. Calvin Colton (New York: Barnes, 1857), 1:433, 476

5. James Madison, Veto of the Bonus Bill, March 3, 1817, in *Writings of Madison*, 8:386.

6. Here and after, James Madison to Andrew Stevenson, November 27, 1830, in *Writings of Madison* 9:411–424. For the argument that Madison saw things entirely differently. He thought that the third generation had gotten the history wrong. They misunderstood the framers' notion of general welfare, see Drew McCoy, *The Last of the Fathers: James Madison and the Republican Legacy* (New York: Cambridge University Press, 1989), 77–78. The problem with this position was that Hamilton was there, and he saw the same language enabling a powerful federal government to make sweeping use of the general-welfare clause.

7. Calhoun quoted in Don E. Fehrenbacher, *Constitutions and Constitutionalism in the Slaveholding South* (Athens: University of Georgia Press, 1989), 47. On Calhoun's moderation, compared to others in the state, see John Niven, *John C. Calhoun and the Price of Union: A Biography* (Baton Rouge: Louisiana State University Press, 1993), 26.

8. Here and after, John C. Calhoun, "Exposition," 1828, in *The Papers of John C. Calhoun*, ed. Clyde N. Wilson and W. Edwin Hemphill (Columbia: University of South Carolina Press, 1977), 10: 445–533.

9. James Madison, Notes on Nullification [1835–1836], *Writings of Madison*, 9:606.

10. Madison, "Advice to My Country" [1834], in Ketcham, ed. *Selected Writings of James Madison*, 362; Nedelsky, *Private Property and the Limits of American Constitutionalism*, 179.

11. Story's son and first biographer, William Wetmore Story, promoted the idea that his father hated slavery. *Life and Letters of Joseph Story* (Boston: Chapman, 1854), 338. Robert Cover, *Justice Accused* (New Haven: Yale University Press, 1984), 241, finds Story much more accommodating in law than he was in his personal views.

12. On Justice Story, the best modern biographies are R. Kent Newmyer, *Supreme Court Justice Joseph Story, Statesman of the Old Republic* (Chapel Hill: University of North Carolina Press, 1985), and Gerald T. Dunne, *Justice Joseph Story and the Rise of the Supreme Court* (New York: Simon and Schuster, 1970).

13. Joseph Story, *Commentaries on the Constitution of the United States*, three volumes (Boston: Hilliard, Gray, 1833), 1:2.

14. *Martin v. Hunter's Lessee*, 14 U.S. 304, 323–324 (1816) (Story, J.).

15. Story, *Commentaries* 1:164,

16. See, e.g., Robert P. Forbes, *The Missouri Compromise and Its Aftermath: Slavery & the Meaning of America* (Chapel Hill: University of North Carolina Press, 2007), 94.

17. Newmyer, *Supreme Court Justice Joseph Story*, 353; Story, *Commentaries* 3:677.

18. Here and after, Story, *Commentaries* 2:367–458; Caleb Nelson, "Originalism and Interpretive Conventions" *University of Chicago Law Review* 70 (2003), 537–538.

19. Story to Ezekiel Bacon, April 8, 1842, *Life and Letters of Joseph Story*, ed. William Whetmore Story (Boston: Little, Brown, 1851), 420; Story to John Brazer, February 11, 1833, ibid., 2:124. Madison's notes had become available in 1840, three years after his death. There is no evidence in the Story or Madison papers that the two men were intimates, and Madison nominated Story to the High Court with some reservations. Kermit Hall, *The Path to and from the Supreme Court* (London: Taylor and Francis, 2000), 183. Story hated the nullifiers and thought nullification would destroy the Constitution. Newmyer, *Story*, 184–185; Story, *Commentaries* 1:166–167.

20. Story, *Commentaries* 1:389.

21. Story, *Commentaries* 2:382.

22. Story, *Commentaries* 1:145.

23. Wendell Phillips, Speech, November 1, 1859; Phillips, Speech, February 1, 1861, in *Wendell Phillips on Civil Rights and Freedom*, ed. Louis Filler (New York: Hill and Wang, 1965), 101, 118; Alexander H. Stephens, "Address to the Georgia Secession Convention," January 18, 1861, in *The*

*Forms of Public Address*, ed. George Pierce Baker (New York: Holt, 1904), 402.

24. See Don E. Fehrenbacher (completed by Ward M. McAfee), *The Slaveholding Republic* (New York: Oxford University Press, 2001), 247–248.

25. *Declaration of the Immediate Causes Which Induce and Justify the Secession of South Carolina from the Federal Union, December 24, 1860* (Charleston, S.C.; n.p. 1860).

26. *Constitution of the Confederate States of America*, March 11, 1861 (Milledgeville, GA: Broughton, 1861). On Cobb's role in the drafting, see Paul Finkelman, "Introduction," in Finkelman, ed., *Thomas R. R. Cobb, An Inquiry into the Law of Negro Slavery in the United States of America* [1858] (Athens: University of Georgia Press, 1999), 5.

27. Allan Kulikoff, *From British Peasants to Colonial American Farmers* (Chapel Hill: University of North Carolina Press, 2000), 292; Richard Bernstein, *The Founding Fathers Reconsidered* (New York: Oxford University Press, 2009), 8.

28. Cobb, *Law of Negro Slavery*, 5.

29. James Buchanan, "State of the Union Message to Congress" December 3, 1860; in Richardson, ed., *Messages of the Presidents*, 5:626; Buchanan, "Message to Congress" January 30, 1861, in Richardson, ed., *Messages of the Presidents*, 5: 663.

30. Abraham Lincoln, January, 1861 [after receiving a December 30, 1860, letter from Alexander H. Stephens?], in Roy P. Basler, ed. *Abraham Lincoln: His Speeches and Writings* (Cleveland: World Publishing, 1946), 513; see also Harold Hyman, *A More Perfect Union* (New York: Knopf, 1973), 132.

31. Here and after, Abraham Lincoln, "Address to Congress," July 4, 1861, in Richardson, ed., *Messages of the Presidents*, 7: 3227–3232.

32. James M. McPherson, *Battle Cry of Freedom: The Civil War Era* (New York: Oxford University Press, 2003), 239; Carl Degler, *The Other Civil South: Southern Dissenters in the Nineteenth Century* (Boston: Northeastern University Press, 1982), 168–170; John Waklyn, *Southern Unionist Pamphlets and the Civil War* (Columbia: University of Missouri Press, 1999), 1–2.

33. Lincoln had little contact with Jefferson Davis, but it is inconceivable that the two presidents were unaware of what each was saying about the Constitution in the early years of the conflict. Davis's message was reprinted in *The New York Times* on May 6, 1861, and Lincoln was an avid newspaper reader. Albert Shaw, *Abraham Lincoln: His Path to the Presidency* (New York, 1929), 27.

34. McPherson, *Battle Cry*, 239, 242, 255.

**Chapter Six**

1. Charles Sumner, "Are We a Nation?" Address to the Young Republican Union at Cooper Institute, November 19, 1867, *Complete Works of Charles Sumner*, ed. George F. Hoar (Boston: Lee and Shepard, 1900), 16:54.

2. Alexander Tsesis, *The Thirteenth Amendment and American Freedom: A Legal History* (New York: New York University Press, 2004), 111, 131; Eric Foner, *Reconstruction: America's Unfinished Revolution, 1863–1877* (New York: Harper and Row, 1988), 67.

3. John Mercer Langston, *Equality Before the Law* (Washington, DC, 1866), 9.

4. Mississippi Code, 1865, in Michael Bellesiles and Christopher Waldrep, eds., *Documenting American Violence: A Sourcebook* (New York: Oxford University Press, 2006), 174–175; David Bacon, *Illegal People: How Globalization Creates Migration and Criminalizes Immigrants* (Boston: Beacon, 2008), 204–205.

5. Civil Rights Act of 1866, 14 Stat. 27–30, April 9, 1866.

6. The story is told in chilling and compelling detail in Charles Lane, *The Day Freedom Died: The Colfax Masscre, the Supreme Court, and the Betrayal of Reconstruction* (New York: Holt, 2007).

7. *U.S. v. Cruikshank* 92 U.S. 542, 559 (1875) (Waite, C.J.).

8. *Plessy v. Ferguson* 163 U.S. 537, 555 (1896) (Harlan, J. dissenting); Jacobson v. Massachusetts 197 U.S. 11, 20–21 (1906) (Harlan J.).

9. David S. Cecelski and Timothy B. Tyson, *Democracy Betrayed: The Wilmington Race Riot of 1898 and Its Legacy* (Chapel Hill: University of North Carolina Press, 1997), 202; Gary Gerstle, "Race and Nation in the Thought and Politics of Woodrow Wilson," in John Milton Cooper, ed. *Reconsidering Woodrow Wilson* (Baltimore: Johns Hopkins University Press, 2008), 110.

10. Hoffer, Hoffer, and Hull, *The Supreme Court: An Essential History*, 252; David M. Kennedy, *Freedom from Fear: The American People in Depression and War, 1929–1945* (New York: Oxford University Press, 2000), 190–248.

11. Alexander Sidney Lanier, "Letter to the Editor," *Washington Post*, April 12, 1933, p. 6; "General Welfare," *New York Times*, November 15, 1935, p. 22.

12. S. Boyd Darling, "Letter to the Editor," *New York Times*, November 17, 1935, p. E9; John J. Jansen, "Letter to the Editor," *New York Times*, November 20, 1935, p. 22; Alfred Lilienthal and David Du Vivier, "Letter to the Editor," *New York Times*, November 30, 1935, p. 14. The letter is full of historical inaccuracies. Hamilton's proposals for funding the national debt, assumption of the state debts, and the creation of a national bank passed Congress and were never reviewed by the High Court. He had no hand in the Alien and Sedition Acts, but the justices of the High Court riding circuit to hear cases under the Seditious Libel Act found it constitutional. The High Court heard a challenge to the Second Bank of the United States in 1819, in *McCulloch v. Maryland* (17 U.S. 316) and

found the bank constitutional, John Marshall using the same arguments that Hamilton had used to argue for the First Bank of the United States.

13. 295 U.S. 495, 531 (1935) (Hughes, C. J.).

14. "General Welfare Urged by Wallace," *New York Times*, December 8, 1935; Attorney General Homer Cummings had outlined the general welfare case in his written brief; "the general welfare clause should be construed broadly to permit the levying of taxes to raise revenue for any purpose conducive to the general welfare." Cummings, quoted in "Welfare Clause Invoked for AAA," *New York Times*, November 19, 1935, p. 5.

15. Stanley Forman Reed's remarks, n.p., preceding the report of *U.S. v. Butler* 297 U.S. 1 (1936).

16. George Wharton Pepper, remarks, ibid.

17. Reed, remarks, ibid.

18. 297 U.S. at 64 (Owen Roberts, J.)

19. Id. at 65.

20. Id. at 66.

21. Hoffer, Hoffer, and Hull, *Supreme Court*, 255; *Korematsu v. U.S.*, 323 U.S. 214, 225 (1945) (Owen Roberts, J.).

22. Here and after, 297 U.S. at 79, 80, 81, 86, 87 (Stone, J.)

23. *Bailey v. Drexel Furniture Co.*, 20, 38 (1922) (Taft, C. J.). Arguing that the Court does hear public opinion: Lucas A. Powe, "The Supreme Court and Election Returns" in Christopher Tomlins, ed., *The United States Supreme Court: The Pursuit of Justice* (Boston: Houghton Mifflin, 2005), 423–445; Peter Irons, *New Deal Lawyers* (Princeton: Princeton University Press, 1993), 279; Jeffrey Rosen, *The Most Democratic Branch: How the Courts Save America* (New York: Oxford University Press, 2006), 7. Contra: Stephen G. Calabresi, "Introduction," in *Originalism: A Quarter Century of Debate* (Chicago: Henry Regnery, 2007), 23–24; Howard Gillman, *Supreme Court Decision Making: New Institutionalist Approaches* (Chicago: University of Chicago Press, 1999), 177.

24. Kennedy, *Freedom from Fear*, 322.

25. Act of August 14, 1935, 49 Stat. 620; Roy Lubove, *The Struggle for Social Security, 1900–1935* (Pittsburgh: University of Pittsburgh Press, 1986), 174–175.

26. Linn Gale, "Letter to the Editor," *Washington Post*, June 16, 1936; Fay Lomax Cook and Edith J. Barrett, *Support for the American Welfare State: The Views of Congress and the Public* (New York: Columbia University Press, 1992), 15; Gary Walton and Hugh Rockoff, *History of the American Economy*, 11th ed. (Florence, KY: Cengage, 2009), 457.

27. *Stewart Sewing Machine Company v. Davis*, 301 U.S. 548, 581, 583, 586–587 (1937) (Cardozo, J.). No need to rehearse here the debate over the shift in the Court's or, actually, Roberts' views between *Butler* and the

1937 cases, in which he sided with the government. Instead, see William E. Leuchtenberg, *The Supreme Court Reborn: The Constitutional Revolution in the Age of Roosevelt* (New York: Oxford University Press, 1995), 213–236 (politics dictated the shift when Roosevelt won a crushing victory in 1936); Barry Cushman, *Rethinking the New Deal Court: The Structure of a Constitutional Revolution* (New York: Oxford University Press, 1998), 156–207 (the basis for the shift was already present before the Court packing plan was announced); G. Edward White, *The Constitution and the New Deal* (Cambridge, MA: Harvard University Press, 2000), 198–239 (currents in doctrine, not political events, led to the shift).

28. Lizabeth Cohen, *Making a New Deal: Industrial Workers in Chicago, 1919–1939*, 2nd ed. (New York: Cambridge University Press, 2008), xix.

29. Martin Luther King Jr., excerpt from "Why We Can't Wait" [1964], reprinted in James M. Washington, ed., *A Testament of Hope: The Essential Writings and Speeches of Martin Luther King Jr.* (New York: Harper Collins, 1991), 525.

## Epilogue: "Our Posterity"

1. Christian Eisgruber, *Constitutional Self-Government* (Cambridge, MA: Harvard University Press, 2001), 11–12; Christian G. Fritz, *American Sovereigns: The People and America's Constitutional Tradition Before the Civil War* (New York: Cambridge University Press, 2009), 289; *Parents Involved in Community Schools v. Seattle School District No. 1*, 551 U.S. 701, 858 (2007) (Breyer, J. diss).

2. Franklin D. Roosevelt, Annual Message to Congress, January 3, 1940, "State of the Union Addresses"; www.infoplease.com/t/hist/state-of-the-union/151.html.

3. President Lyndon Johnson's message was reported in the *New York Times* July 3, 1964, p. 1.

4. Peter Rodino and Charles Black, quoted in Eric M. Axler, "The Power of the Preamble and the Ninth Amendment," *Seton Hall Legislative Journal* 24 (2000), 434–437.

5. *Gregory et al. v. City of Chicago*, 394 U.S. 111, 113 (1969) (Black, J. concurring).

6. *District of Columbia v. Heller*, 554 U.S. 570, 578 n.3 (Scalia, J.) (2008); *McDonald v. City of Chicago*, 561 U.S. 3025 (2010). On the two cases and the dispute over the role of preambles, see Lawrence Rosenthal and Joyce Lee Malcolm, "McDonald v. Chicago: Which Standard of Scrutiny Should Apply to Gun Control Laws" *Northwestern University Law Review* 105 (2010), 85–114, but this is just the tip of the iceberg of legal commentary on the two cases.

7. Barack Obama, "A More Perfect Union," *The Black Scholar* 38 (2008), 17; R. B. Bernstein, *Founding Fathers*, 169.

# FOR FURTHER READING

...................

A comprehensive listing of suggested further readings on the Preamble in American history would consume more pages than I have used to tell the tale in this book. Making the listing more complicated, the subject is one that interests political scientists and jurists as well as historians. For these reasons, I have elected to include here only books that I can recommend without hesitation for their contribution to the field, their readability, and their centrality to my story. Additional readings are cited in the endnotes. Note as well that any list, and the list herein is certainly no exception, will lean a little in the direction of the scholarly compiler's own take on the subject.

Many of the primary sources—contemporary documents, letters, diaries, published debates and pamphlets—are now available in digital form. Some remain in letter press editions only. Publishers of books, librarians, and purveyors of electronic websites are trying to sort out among themselves when and how much of work still in copyright should be digitized. The major sources remain the *Journals of the Continental Congress* (Washington, DC: U.S. Government Printing Office, 1904–1937), 31 vols.; the three volumes of Max Farrand, ed., *Records of the Federal Convention of 1787* (New Haven: Yale University Press, 1911), supplemented by a fourth volume of letters (1966); and the fifteen volumes and counting of Merrill Jensen and John Kaminski, eds., *Documentary History of the Ratification of the Constitution* (Madison: Wisconsin Historical Society, 1976–). Electronic sources include "The Founders' Constitution," a Web resource prepared by the University of Chicago Press and the Liberty Fund, edited by Philip B. Kurland and Ralph Lerner, http://press-pubs.uchicago.edu/founders; and various editions of the *Federalist Papers*. Older editions and some portions of more recent editions of the papers of some of the leading figures in the framing have also been digitized, including Alexander Hamilton, Thomas Jefferson, Abraham Lincoln, James Madison, and George Washington. Full citations to these appear in the endnotes. In general, recent editions are far more trustworthy, accurate, and better annotated than their nineteenth-century predecessors, but as of this writing, the Jefferson and Madison papers recent editions are incomplete.

The method of interpreting the Constitution as well as the meaning of any of its portions is a hotly contested three-way battle among originalists (trying to find out what the framers really wanted), plain text advocates (trying to interpret the language in its plainest way), and defenders of the idea of a living constitution (arguing that the framers wanted each generation to apply its own meanings to their words). On the origins of this controversy, see Alan Gibson, *Interpreting the Founding: Guide to the Enduring Debates over the Origins and Foundations of the American Republic*, 2nd ed. (Lawrence: University Press of Kansas, 2009) and Jonathan G. O'Neill, *Originalism in American Law and Politics: A Constitutional History* (Baltimore: Johns Hopkins University Press, 2007). The classic work on the controversy is Leonard Levy, *Original Intent and the Framers' Constitution* (New York: Macmillan, 1988). Defenses of originalism are collected in Antonin Scalia and Stephen G. Calabresi, eds., *Originalism: A Quarter Century of Debate* (New York: Regnery, 2007). Other valuable contributions to the debate, all with an eye on history, are Akhil Amar, *America's Constitution: A Biography* (New York: Random House, 2005); Edward A. Purcell, *Originalism, Federalism and the American Constitutional Enterprise: A Historical Inquiry* (New Haven: Yale University Press, 2007), and Jack Rakove, *Original Meanings: Politics and Ideas in the Making of the Constitution* (New York: Knopf, 1996).

On the years of war and political uncertainty from 1775 to 1787, the standard work is Richard B. Morris, *The Forging of the Union* (New York: Harper, 1987), but see also Rakove, *The Beginnings of National Politics: An Interpretive History of the Continental Congress* (Baltimore: Johns Hopkins University Press, 1982). More controversial are Woody Holton's lively *Unruly Americans and the Origins of the Constitution* (New York: Hill and Wang, 2007), and, on the other side of the ideological street, Gordon S. Wood's *The Creation of the American Republic, 1776–1787* (Chapel Hill: University of North Carolina Press, 1969) and *The Radicalism of the American Revolution* (New York: Knopf, 1992).

Recent and very accessible accounts of the Constitutional Convention and the drafting of the Constitution include Richard Beeman, *Plain, Honest Men: The Making of the American Constitution* (New York: Random House, 2009); Carol Berkin, *Brilliant Solution: Inventing the American Constitution* (New York: Harcourt, 2002); David O. Stewart, *The Summer of 1787: The Men Who Invented the Constitution* (New York: Simon and Schuster, 2007); and Rakove, *Original Meanings*. A very useful encyclopedia is John R. Vile, ed., *The Constitutional Convention of 1787: A Comprehensive Encyclopedia*, 2 volumes (Santa Barbara, CA: ABC-Clio, 2005).

Narrower topics in this portion of the story include law practice and the framers, for which see Peter Charles Hoffer, *Law and People in Colonial America*,

2nd ed. (Baltimore: Johns Hopkins University Press, 1998); the tribulations of Valley Forge, on which see Wayne K. Bodle, *The Valley Forge Winter: Civilians and Soldiers in War* (State College: Pennsylvania State University Press, 2004); the troubled diplomacy of the new nation, tracked in Reginald Horsman, *The Diplomacy of the New Republic, 1776–1815* (Arlington Heights, IL: Davidson, 1985); on the problems of the confederacy, noted in Peter Onuf, *The Origins of the Federal Republic: Jurisdictional Controversies in the United States, 1775–1787* (Philadelphia: University of Pennsylvania Press, 1983); on Shays's Rebellion, for which see David Szatmary, *Shays' Rebellion: The Making of an Agrarian Insurrection* (Amherst: University of Massachusetts Press, 1980) and Leonard L. Richards, *Shays Rebellion: The American Revolution's Final Battle* (Philadelphia: University of Pennsylvania Press, 2004).

The new gold standard on the ratification process is Pauline Maier, *Ratification: The People Debate the Constitution, 1787–1788* (New York: Simon and Schuster, 2010). More didactic contributions to the literature include Saul Cornell, *The Other Founders: Anti-Federalism and the Dissenting Tradition in America, 1788– 1828* (Chapel Hill: University of North Carolina Press, 1999), Max M. Edling, *A Revolution in Favor of Government: Origins of the U.S. Constitution and the Making of the American State* (New York: Oxford University Press, 2003), and Jackson Turner Main, *The Antifederalists* (Chapel Hill: University of North Carolina Press, 1961).

On the tumultuous politics of the 1790s, see Eric L. McKitrick and Stanley M. Elkins's magisterial *The Age of Federalism* (New York: Oxford University Press, 1993). See also James Roger Sharp, *American Politics in the Early Republic: The New Nation in Crisis* (New Haven: Yale University Press, 1993), and a now often overlooked gem, Joseph Charles, *The Origins of the American Party System* (Williamsburg, VA: Colonial Williamsburg, 1956).

The debate over the Sedition Act and the issuance of the Virginia and Kentucky resolutions is well covered in James Morton Smith, *Freedom's Fetters: The Alien and Sedition Laws and American Civil Liberties* (Ithaca, NY: Cornell University Press, 1956) and Peter Charles Hoffer, *The Free Press Crisis of 1800: Thomas Cooper's Trial for Seditious Libel* (Lawrence: University Press of Kansas, 2010).

Nullification and secession were constitutional doctrines according to their proponents: see Don E. Fehrenbacher, *Constitutions and Constitutionalism in the Slaveholding South* (Athens: University of Georgia Press, 1989), Fehrenbacher, *Sectional Crisis and Southern Constitutionalism* (Baton Rouge: Louisiana State University Press, 1995), and John Niven, *John C. Calhoun and the Price of Union* (Baton Rouge: Louisiana State University Press, 1988). On Lincoln and the Union, see Harold Holzer, *Lincoln President-Elect: Abraham Lincoln and the Great Secession Winter, 1860–1861* (New York: Simon and Schuster, 2008), Harold Hyman, *A More Perfect Union: The Impact of the Civil War and Reconstruction on the Constitution* (New York: Knopf, 1973), and Mark E. Neely, *Lincoln and the Triumph of the Nation: Constitutional Conflict in the American Civil War* (Chapel Hill: University of North Carolina Press, 2011).

# INDEX

........................